William Stephenson, PhD

TEACHABLE MOMENTS

Lessons to Enrich Our Mental Health, Our Spiritual Journey and Our Relationships

William Stephenson Books

www.williamstephensonbooks.com

stephenson2789@gmail.com

Contents

PREFACE

As I gave particular attention to clients facing a life-threatening illness, I discovered that there were some common elements of concern they wanted to address. In addition to discovering how to cope with a life-threatening illness, they also had personal and relational issues they wanted to reconcile while they were still able.

Most of these concerns were drawn into this book. As the book took shape, it was apparent that the topics it would address were common to what many of us will encounter. Except my clients were running out of time.

One of the reasons for this book is to offer some suggestions that can be applied to what I call "roadblocks to wholeness." Once I had identified what these issues were, I began to lead a group of "fellow travelers" on a journey through each of these chapters.

However, the "elephant in the room" was the act of forgiveness. I have given this issue its own section because it was so dominating in our brokenness and alienation. But the other two sections, "Days When…" and "Our Mental and Spiritual Health" will likely touch upon concerns you or someone important in your life has been wrestling with.

In most chapters I offer a scripture reference (NRSV) as well as questions to consider journaling or sharing in a group. But every chapter is to bring you to a better understanding of your relationship to God and to those on this planet.

All the best on your journey.

Hope is the companion of power and mother of success;
for who so hopes strongly has within him the gift of miracles
—Samuel Smiles

SECTION ONE:
Forgiveness

In joined hands there is still some token of hope.

In the clenched fists There is none.

—Victor Hugo

INTRODUCTION

One of the most challenging tasks we humans have can be found in the realm of forgiveness. It often requires us to confront deep emotions, reflect honestly on our experiences, and open ourselves to the possibility of transformation.

Whether the wounds are recent or long-standing, the process of forgiving is rarely straightforward and can test our resolve and understanding.

Forgiveness is like dancing. Specific rules need to be followed for I to be genuine forgiveness. But, like dancing, be prepared to step on toes and apologize for not doing it right.

Most of us are self-taught when it comes to the art of forgiving. But when we do it right, like dancing, it is indeed a teachable moment.

This section on forgiveness will challenge you to address when and how to participate in this new dance we call "forgiveness."

At the end of each chapter, I have offered a scripture that may reveal even more of ourselves. Because it's not who we are, but whose we are.

CHAPTER ONE

Forgiveness is Hard Work

Forgiveness is hard work. Why?

It is hard, first of all, when forgiveness is given as a way of denying that there is any anger or any hurt. This is often because we were taught that the speed of forgiving was more important than the pain and hurt experienced in the offense. This kind of forgiveness cannot be trusted. It's a fantasy.

Second, it's also hard to forgive because we often keep this hurt alive by resentment after identifying it. Resentment means "to feel again." When we have been hurt, resentment is our way of feeling it repeatedly. Resentment keeps the hurt fresh and alive.

Third, forgiveness is hard work because we often trick ourselves into believing that revenge gets things even. We have a way of keeping revenge alive for the loftiest reasons: "It's a matter of principle." "I must not be too easy on him." "She's only getting what she was asking for." "He's just getting what he deserves." "There are days when I just want to scream!" This is what one of my clients said in a counseling session. Not just a day here and there but many days. Have you ever had a day like that—when you just wanted to scream? *Teachable Moments* series came into being from that profound question. Unfortunately, for some, the days turned into weeks, and some even into months. These include revenge, anxiety, and self-esteem, and the list grew, as did lessons on other ways we try to cope with those "screaming" days.

Each Teachable Moment chapter addresses the human condition and how our mental health and faith are challenged. You will begin to see how the "recovery model" is applied. The emphasis is on teaching ourselves not to deal with these issues alone but to trust one or more persons with those "days" and to remind ourselves that God is always with us through the journey of "days when." And, last, this force called forgiveness is not so much what it does for the other person but what forgiving does for ourselves Is that the pain becomes manageable and ceases to be what defines us. It gives a new way to live again, love again and that's what makes the angels sing.

Suggested scripture: Isaiah 11:1–10

Questions for Journaling and Conversation

1. Can you recall when you could not relinquish the need to get even?
2. How do you handle the burden of pain when the offender is dead?
3. For forgiveness to occur, what must the other person do?

CHAPTER TWO

The Unforgivable

Among the many patients I have counseled, there was one who believed that he had committed an unforgivable sin. Consequently, he judged that nothing could be done to help him. This was the first time I was confronted with the fact that when something that big and complex can go so deep into the subconscious, no therapy can reach it. When people such as this client genuinely believe they have done something so unforgivable that they are eternally condemned, they are both spiritually and mentally ill.

To ask the question "Is there an unforgivable sin?" is to deal with a highly emotional question, so psychologically crucial that it is destructive to deal with it unless one puts it back into its context, the original setting in which Jesus first said it (Mark 3:20-29). Take a few moments and read the scripture provided as Jesus confronts the "unforgivable."

What is so unforgivable? This analogy. You hear of children in a particular town starving for food. You reach out to them, and you rent a big truck and fill it with good food. You drive it to where these starving children are located, and just as they are about to eat some of the food you brought to them, leaders in the town come and say to the children, "Stop! That food is poisonous! Eat it, and you will get very sick and die!" And the children, trusting their leaders, don't eat the food and continue to starve. And every time you return with food for them to eat, the leaders say to the children, "Stop! Don't eat that food! It's poisonous!" And the leaders say this lie so often that even they begin to believe it.

The unforgivable sin is when you begin to believe in your own lies. To tell a lie so often, one starts to think it's not a lie, but it's indeed righteous to say it. So, who needs forgiveness? One cannot be forgiven for something one does not ask forgiveness for.

But the problem with this scripture about unforgivable sin is that the wrong people worry that they may have committed it. Someone reading this may feel deep in one's subconscious that there is something to feel guilty about and it is impossible to be forgiven for it.

During the AIDS crisis, I was accepting many more patients in my care. I decided to start group sessions, hoping that would relieve me of the overwhelming demand for individual and couples counseling. I underestimated the demand, and one planned group of eight became four groups of six to eight. All of them were facing only months with end-of-life issues. None of them had any support systems, family, or church participation. All of them were hoping that this group could become their surrogate family. And for many of them, it did.

At one session of one of the groups, I came in late for the second time. All of them were waiting. As I began apologizing, one older man interrupted me and said, "Dr. Bill, we need this group because we have no one else to turn to. But we also don't want this to burden you, and we sense that you seem distressed and disengaging. You are the one well person in our lives, and we can't afford that. This group has become a life force for us, but we think you need to have this group."

With tears in my eyes, I took a breath and nodded. "You all have so much on your plate. I didn't want to be a distraction. But I think I'm in over my head!" And then we began to share like no other time before.

That was the conflict that Jesus had with the Pharisees. The Pharisees were teaching people that they were burdens to God and had to follow their way or God would never love or accept them.

But Jesus dared with His own life to confront that and say, "No, you're never a burden to God. You are the light of the world. You are God's blessing."

For someone reading this, and with that gnawing guilt, that you have committed an unforgivable sin, begin today to believe with all your heart and mind that you are not a burden to God. To claim that place is to turn unforgivable into a peace that passes all understanding.

Our faith and our mental health are so intertwined. To feel unforgiven is such a burden to yourself and others. But listen to Jesus's message amid the yelling that there is room in God's realm that includes even a wretch like you: accepted, loved, understood. Forgiven.

When you allow that message to get deep into your mind, heart, and soul, that healing you hunger for will begin. And the peace and wholeness, often beyond our understanding, will be yours.

Suggested scripture: Mark 3:20–29

Questions for Journaling and Conversation

1. Describe a time or event that you felt was unforgivable.
2. Given the recent violence in places like Ukraine, how does one reconcile with the perpetrators?
3. Is there any act or behavior you judge God would not forgive?
4. What must you do to get to a place where you can forgive?

"The best way to not feel hopeless
is to get up and do something.
Don't wait for good things to happen to you.
If you go out and make some good things happen,
you will fill the world with hope,
you will fill yourself with hope."
—Barack Obama

CHAPTER THREE:
Healing Through Words

> "Which is easier, to say to the paralytic, 'Your sins are forgiven,' or to say, 'Stand up and take your mat and walk'? But so that you may know the Son of Man has authority on earth to forgive sins," he said to the paralytic, "I say to you, stand up, take your mat and go to your home." And he stood up and immediately took the mat and went out before all of them; so that they were all amazed and glorified God, saying, "We have never seen anything like this!" (Mark 2:9–12 [NRSV])

This scripture is a story about healing through words. Jesus doesn't touch the man. He says something. Jesus merely passes the information on to the patient, and it makes all the difference.

The second thing that emerges from this story is that we all have a way with words. When Jesus says, "Your sins are forgiven," the scribes scream foul. They call it "blasphemy!" And they accuse Jesus of blasphemy because they believe, and want everyone else to think, that only God has the authority to forgive sins. And Jesus confronts this belief. And the people are amazed that God has given this authority to all—that we all have a way with words.

There are times when you and I are the only ones who can forgive someone. No one else can do our forgiving in a relationship. Not even God. No wonder the crowd around Jesus was amazed and afraid when He said to the man, "Your sins are forgiven."

In our nation, over a million children are runaways every year. Over a hundred thousand children's bodies end up in the city morgues unclaimed, buried unnamed every year. The third leading cause of death for children from six to sixteen is suicide. In a classified column, the personal ad read, "Dear Son. Please come home. Your father forgives you." Signed, "Mom." But the boy needed to hear his dad say it. No one else can do our forgiving for us.

Jesus suggests that God gives everyone authority to use words to heal. Our terms can lift or tear down, destroy or heal, but they will communicate one way or another. What a privilege. What a responsibility.

The third thing this story does is it comes with a terrible confrontation with something very close to me, and that's my way of relating.

I have been trained and taught to believe that recovery comes only when there's some requirement for behavior modification. First, you change your behavior, and then we'll talk about acceptance, forgiveness, and reconciliation.

"If I give you forgiveness and accept you before you change your behavior, then I may be condoning your behavior, and cheapens the whole thing: Now, you change the way the way you're doing things, and then I'll change my attitude toward you."

Isn't that the more enlightened way? And yet Jesus does precisely the opposite. He says, "Your sins are forgiven." He never talks about any behavior change.

Read the record. Jesus's message can be found in each one of the Gospels. In John, when they bring the woman taken in adultery to Jesus, the first words to her are, "Your sins are forgiven." Then, he talks about behavioral change.

Jesus put it more clearly in another setting. He said, quoting Proverbs, "As a man thinketh in his heart, so is he." In other words, the image you and I have of ourselves determines our behavior. And that's what Jesus went about, first starting not with people's behavior but the image they had of themselves.

That's why acceptance is so crucial. Jesus lifted their self-image. He said, "Why, you're the light of the world. You're not what they say you are. You're the salt of the earth." Change your image of yourself, and then you'll change your behavior.

Well, what do you think it is? Is it easier to say, "Your sins are forgiven," or "Get up and walk"? Often, you and I will withhold forgiveness because we want to use forgiveness as a way of bartering for change. "I won't forgive you until you do it differently. And it doesn't work. If you're a parent, you know that. What that usually brings is not change but r-e-s-e-n-t-m-e-n-t. And deeply so.

Where is it with you in your relationship with that person you may be out of sorts with or in alienation? We have a way with words. Sometimes, it will be just a word of gratitude that will make all the difference in another person's life. Or maybe a word of forgiveness could change the burden of guilt that someone is carrying.

Perhaps you read that beautiful novel by Ann Morrow Lindbergh called *Dearly Beloved*. She describes a problem that takes place with the mother at the wedding of her daughter. And while she's waiting for her daughter to become a bride, she imagines her relationship with all the different people at the wedding party. She looks at her daughter and says to herself, *I hope that all her life she will be able to share with her husband the ribbons and not just the strings.*

And then she looks at her husband and says to herself, We don't share the ribbons anymore, just the strings. The grocery store strings. And she muses about how that happened. She said, When we were first married, and he would come home at the end of the day, I would tell him everything I did and thought that day. And he would pounce on my mistakes like my old arithmetic teacher and say, "Why you did this wrong, and that wrong, and this was wrong …" until I no longer shared the ribbons. Just the strings.

The hurt, lack of love, and joy from our relationships are because we do not use healing words. We share only the strings. But God has given us the power and the authority to differently." And it doesn't work. If you're a parent, you know share the ribbons. To say to someone you value, "All

13

is forgiven," is a ribbon you will both wear with gratitude. Your words enriched both of your lives.

Questions for Journaling or Conversation

1. Can you recall when your words brought healing and hope?
2. Before you commit to the problem, do you try to define the problem?
3. Can you recall when you "ransomed" your forgiveness?

We must accept finite disappointment
but never lose infinite hope.
—Martin Luther King, Jr.

CHAPTER FOUR

What does God know?

I offer this parable that needs no explanation.

In the beginning, God put us all in the Garden or, call it a playground. God said, "Now, I want you to enjoy yourselves. Have fun!" And we had fun! We rolled down the hills, we waded in the streams, we climbed the trees, we ran across the meadows, we hid in the forest, we enjoyed ourselves, and we had fun. We would pause every once in a while, and we would say, "What a great, good God we have to give us a garden like this. Aren't we having fun?"

Then along came Snake. And Snake said, "You're not having real fun."

We said, "Yes, we are."

"No, you're not having real fun because you don't know who is the best."

Snake said, "No, you really won't know who is the best unless you keep score. So, here's what you do. You take an apple, like a trophy, and you give it to the person who's best, and the one who gets the most apples, the most trophies, is the best and the winner."

We tried it. But if we were going to keep score, we had to have rules. We took our games and started making rules and keeping score. And do you remember how we started yelling and criticizing each other? We couldn't play in some games anymore because we couldn't keep score.

God was upset and said, "That's not what I intended when I gave you this garden. You were to enjoy yourselves. But you're keeping score, and you're comparing and competing, and you're fighting. You have to leave the garden, and you can't return until you stop keeping score."

We said, "God, you just don't know. We really are having fun!"

But God said, "Your scorekeeping doesn't mean anything!" Then, to rub it in, and that's what God does when God wants to get our attention, God said, "You know, you're all going to die anyway, and your scores aren't going to mean anything."

Well, what did God know? My score means a lot to me. My all-time accumulative score is exactly 16,455. I'm hoping that by the time I die, l will reach 30,000! Then I will die knowing that I've accomplished something!

Occasionally, I have to peek over at Jane's score to see who's better, and that throws me off guard. But even if I don't reach 30,000, my life is still going to account for something because I'm teaching my children how to keep score! Maybe, just maybe, by the time they die, they'll have reached 30,000, and then my life will have been all worthwhile.

God said, "Don't keep score. Enjoy yourself." But what does God know?

So, we keep our scores. We keep track of every resentment, every grudge, every put-down, every disappointment, every slight. And where do we put them? Our emotions say, "We've got a place. Put all those right here in your body." And the body takes all of that in. We claim to have an armor to keep us from being hurt, but it doesn't protect us. Not really.

Scorekeeping. It's our national pastime. It has become a religion. But what does God know?[1]

CHAPTER FIVE

Forgiveness and Hope Reunited

T his scripture for this teachable moment:

> Now Joseph was governor over the land; he sold to all the
> people of the land. And Joseph's brothers came and bowed
> themselves before him with their faces to the ground.
> When Joseph saw his brothers, he recognized them, but
> he treated them like strangers and spoke harshly to them.
> (Gen. 42:6–7)

As we come to the concluding chapter on forgiveness, we draw
upon a counselor's notebook, a sacred verse that kept me very busy as a
therapist: "Joseph saw his brothers and knew them, but he treated them
like strangers." What hope can we squeeze out of that? Do you remember
playing the game, "If You Were God?"

Fathers and mothers have to play that all the time. For example, how
did you teach your children to be considerate? How did you teach your
children what is forgivable and not forgivable. How did you teach your
children the difference between right and wrong? How did you teach your
children the difference between love and hate, trust and fear?

We grow up in a human family, and as fathers and mothers, we must
constantly be playing "If You Were God." Our kids learned kindness and
caring, contempt, dependence, and codependence.

I delivered two of my three children at home. I remember that moment
when I cut the umbilical cord. Isn't that a strange word? *Umbilical* in Latin

means "center"; God says we all start with a center. But even though we cut that cord, there's an invisible cord that cannot be cut, and that cord is memory and meaning, and you're going to learn everything through that.

And who will be in the family playing "If You Were God" but the father? In this family, our center, we will learn the best and the worst. "Joseph saw his brothers, and he treated them like strangers."

The second thing I have in my counselor's notes is how easy it is to treat those in our family as strangers. The Bible suggests that the most meaningful thing they can do with each other is to eat together. The meal was a symbol of being together. But in our culture, how many families sit together every night or day and share a meal? And if they do, without their cell phones or the TV.

We are a culture that has lost the ritual of unity. We are strangers in our homes because no one teaches us the value of breaking bread together and sharing their lives. And we use it as punishment, don't we? "No dinner for you tonight!" or "Take your dinner to your room." Solitary confinement is not just in our prisons.

I had an eighty-three-year-old client who was going to die in this nursing home. As with many of my clients who were terminally ill, my task was to get to them, not them to me. Mr. Patterson was very depressed and lonely, and no one signed his guest book even though he had three children and several grandchildren.

"Well, Mr. Patterson, what are you in for?"

"Old age," he said.

"When was the last time you ate a meal with someone?"

"I can't remember."

From then on, I always came when dinner was served, and we ate together. How easy it is to treat those we know as strangers.

So, where's the hope? In a class I teach weekly, most, if not all, of our fathers have died. It's a different kind of remembrance. Perhaps that may be one reason the Parable of the Prodigal Son is so meaningful. I prefer to call this parable the Parable of the Waiting Father. There is this hunger to find this kind of father in our lives—a forgiving and welcoming and understanding father figure.

In the motion picture *Tribute*, Jack Lemon portrayed a middle-aged father and his frustrating attempt to get closer to his twenty-one-year-old son. But they can't seem to understand each other. They can't communicate or accept each other. They spend what the father knows is his last summer of life with each other because the father was dying.

But nothing seems to work, and, finally, in an explosion of temper, the father looks at his son and says, "You keep telling me that I haven't been the father you wanted! Has it ever occurred to you that you might not be the son I've always wanted?"[2]

Expectations. I don't know how many fathers I have heard them say to their children in my office, "Until you have my full approval of what you are doing with your life, I will not embrace you." Not much chance there of hugging them and throwing a party.

Again, where is the hope? It comes when we stop playing the "If I Were God" game. It comes when we stop with the expectations. It comes when we can seek forgiveness or when we give forgiveness. That's in my therapist's notes. But the truth is in this story.

Randy was brought into the hospice one day before his fifty-eighth birthday. When Randy was admitted, he was angry, hostile, abrupt, and restless. When he was asleep, he would moan as if something wrong had happened.

When asked if everything was OK, he wouldn't answer. The staff knew that he had some unfinished business that he had to deal with if he was to have a "good death."

His physical signs were rapidly deteriorating, but he wouldn't die. He wouldn't let go. It was as if something deep within him would not permit death.

I talked to his son to see if he knew what it was. From the expression on his face, I knew that a family secret was about to be revealed. He said, "I'm not his only child. He has a daughter in Boston. My dad disowned her nine years ago because she married someone of another race. From his point of view, she had committed an unpardonable sin. He said he would never forgive her."

I then knew what his unfinished business was all about. I contacted his daughter and urged her to get to the hospice as fast as possible. Several hours later, she arrived.

For the first time in nine years, he saw his daughter. He said nothing. He just stared at her. Then he opened his arms to his daughter, and, with all the strength he had left in his life, he hugged her. She brushed away his tears as well as her own. She sat on his bed, and neither said anything for the longest time.

Finally, he looked into her eyes and said the words that freed him forever: "I'm sorry. Please forgive me."

There were many more tears. They held one another and talked about old times. He learned that he was now a grandfather, and there were pictures to see, and there was much laughter.

That night, his vital signs were stable and strong. But then an amazing thing began to happen. At around eleven thirty, he said he was tired but didn't want his children to leave. Each child held one of his hands, and he let go.

The bitterness was gone from his face. All his unfinished business had been put to rest. It was a good death. I looked at my watch, and a new day had begun. It was Sunday. It was Father's Day.

Questions for Journaling and Conversation

1. What do you think are the expectations your parents had about you?
2. Did you achieve any of those expectations?
3. What has your experience been with Mother's Day and Father's Day?

SECTION TWO:
Days When…

Hope is a thing of feathers, that perches in the soul,

and sings the tune without the words and never stops at all.

—Emily Dickenson

INTRODUCTION

"There are days when I just want to scream!" This is what one of my clients said in a counseling session. Not just a day here and there but many days. Have you ever had a day like that—when you just wanted to scream?

This *Teachable Moments* series came into being from that profound question. I began to think about the challenging "days when …"

Unfortunately, for some, the days turned into weeks, and some even into months. These include revenge, anxiety, and self-esteem, and the list grew, as did lessons on other ways we try to cope with those "screaming" days.

Each teachable moment addresses the human condition and how our mental health and faith are challenged. You will begin to see how the "recovery model" is applied. The emphasis is on teaching ourselves not to deal with these issues alone but to trust one or more persons with those "days" and to remind ourselves that God is always with us through the journey of "days when."

Enjoy the read. Keep your personal journal close.

CHAPTER SIX:

Days When...
Things Do Not Go Well

W hat do you do when you hear that one of your children is diagnosed with a life-threatening disease, your job is phased out, someone close to you dies, or you have a difficult decision to make and feel all alone with it? What do you do? Do you panic? Implode? Detach yourself? Run away in fear and trembling? What do you do?

When you are having one of those days when things aren't going well, how can you cope with such a day? These don't always work, but I have discovered five handles we can grab hold of when things don't go well. First, find a quiet place for half an hour and do nothing. How often do we hear the advice, "Don't just stand there, do something!" And there are those kinds of emergencies where we have to respond. But not always. Especially when we've suffered some emotional shock or disappointment, that's the time to find a quiet place, breathe deeply, and let your body become calm. How many times do we make decisions in a moment of panic? Take time to settle your emotions.

The second thing to do on days like this is to remind yourself that while you are unique, what you are going through is not. Others have faced these difficult days. What you are facing is not unusual.

In our journeys, we have our hilltops of times when we are happy and healthy. But there are at least four valleys that every human being will walk into at any length of time. Every one of us will experience "disappointment." We're all going to know "defeat." You don't have to live long to become acquainted with "disease." And every one of us has a date with "death."

We will all walk in those valleys, but our path is heavily traveled. Thus, we can say, "I am unique, but what I'm facing is not unique." Remembering that can keep us from resenting and crying out to the heavens, "Why me?" Well, why not you? How easy it is to make ourselves a victim. But while we are unique, our problems are not uncommon. Others have been here before us.

The third thing we can do on days not going well is to remind ourselves that not only have others experienced this kind of day, but they have also gotten through it to tell about it. Remember that no matter how much pain you may be in, the doors to the future are not closed.

Focus on your possibilities instead of dwelling on your difficulties. Each of us has unique skills and qualities that can be used to confront and overcome any handicap or crisis we face. Look in the mirror and say, "I don't know how I will handle this, but I will. I don't know where to find help, but I will find it. I don't know when or where, but it will come from unexpected places. Somehow, someway, help is going to rise up in me."

And that's the fourth thing—to say, "I don't know how I'm going to handle this, but I will." Too often, we commune with what defeats us. We brood over our handicaps. It's attitudinal. When we focus on the possibilities, we become more sensitive and receptive to the resources all about us. Many of whom have been there all the time. But now we have "new eyes" to see them. Here, we can say, "I don't know how I'm going to handle this, but I will." Then, we become more sensitive and open to the resources about us. Now, we are ready for the fifth and final step. Take a few moments and quiet your soul. Pray. In a sense, you have been praying all along.

You have been looking at your situation in God's presence, which is to pray. You were quiet for a while so that you could become calm. You have told yourself *I am unique, but this problem is not unusual.* And, in saying this repeatedly, you have drained yourself of some of the bitterness and defeat.

We have seen that the universe does not select you as a particular target for some problems. Nothing has happened to you that hasn't happened to others. And you have focused on the possibilities you have available.

Then you can say with the Apostle Paul, "I am afflicted in every way, but I am not crushed." You have strengthened yourself through Christ to do what must be done to get through that day when things are not going well.

Suggested scripture: 2 Corinthians 4:1–10

Questions for Journaling and Conversations

1. What other "handles" have you found helpful when facing difficult days?
2. How would you describe a day not going well?
3. Clarify what Paul means in the metaphorical phrase "treasure in clay jars."
4. How often do you start your day by giving thanks to God for gifting you this new day?

Hope is the patient and trustful willingness
to live without closure, without resolution,
and still be content and even happy
because our Satisfaction and now at another level
and our Source is beyond ourselves.
—Richard Rohr

CHAPTER SEVEN

Days When...
You Come to a Dead End

In the scripture listed below, Isaiah learns that power has limitations. As the Jewish people are allowed to return to their homeland, Israel, he discovers that the current generation is resistant. They've settled into Babylon and see no reason to return to a nation in ruins.

This brings us to our journey of power. When God chose to treat us as natural persons, to give us freedom, God made us so that we cannot order people to provide us with the things we most want from them, which can break our hearts.

Yet we attempt to exert power over them in one way or another so that we win and they lose. Win/lose relationships. The surest way to ruin a relationship, frustrate a friendship, or make a mess of a marriage is to insist that someone will win and the other will lose.

But a victory over someone we love is a meaningless one. The very things we want most from each other cannot be won, cannot be demanded, cannot be ordered. And to impose that kind of power over someone you love will break your heart and the spirit of the other.

That's the insight Isaiah discovered. He couldn't force his people to leave Babylon and return. So, he showed the people who did return with him a recovery of purpose rather than an increase in power—to rebuild the temple and rebuild the city. He said, "Let us prepare a way for our people to return. Build a highway. Let us prepare a way for our people to return. Cast the stones out of the way. We will have a recovery of purpose. Let us show our love for them." They did that, and the people returned. Love, not power, rebuilt the nation.

"God so loved the world." Love, not power, would bring us home. God sent one who would prepare the way, who would build us a highway and not a dead-end street, who would cast away the stones, who would raise the banner that this is the grace of God, who made goodness attractive, who gave us a recovery of purpose.

We didn't understand Him, so we put Him on a cross. But before He went there, He said, "If I am lifted even on the cross, I will still draw, not by force, but by love."

You may be in a similar struggle. You can't understand what's happening and why things are going wrong with someone close to you. If only they would see and agree with your way of handling it. But that's power, not love.

Take a moment and focus on someone you are out of sorts and experiencing alienation with, where a vital bridge is broken, and stones litter the highway between you and this other person. What can you do this week to show love for that person and not power over them? Let that miracle of the cross's redemptive power occur again.

Suggested scripture: Isaiah 62:1–4, 8–11

Questions for Journaling and Conversation

1. How has control influenced your life's development so far? How has love?
2. When you and someone you care about disagree, is there something you can do differently?

CHAPTER EIGHT

Days When…
You Are Living in Neutral

One of the most difficult questions we humans have to face and even whole nations must address is: "When you are facing a crisis, how fast should a decision be made? Should a decision be made suddenly, or, should the decision be made slowly and cautiously? When you are facing a crisis, how fast should you make a decision?

First of all, the most challenging work in the world is to decide. The picture of a wholly demolished car was on the front page of the San Francisco Chronicle. Under the picture was the caption "Indecision and Death," then this story:

"Heading into San Francisco from the Golden Gate Bridge Wednesday night, Mr. Ivan Goodman, Age. 51, reached the abutment dividing the Moreno and Civic Center approaches. 'He apparently couldn't decide,' the officer said. And in his indecision, he drove his car into the abutment. Goodman died in the crash."[3]

What an accurate diagnosis of the awful anxiety we feel when we can't make up our minds! The pain of indecision. The power to choose may also be the heaviest burden we carry. The most challenging work in the world is to decide.

Second, because decision-making is such hard work, we tend to develop a tremendous appetite for ready-made answers. The uncertainty of our self-confidence can be so disturbing and upsetting that we're willing to make up our minds long before we've made up our lives! And then we often discover, sometimes too late, that what we ruled out was far more precious than what we walled in! What we didn't know turned out to be more important than what we did know!

If we run through life with ready-made answers, with our minds made up, how often will we discover that what we didn't know turned out to be more important than what we did know? Ready-made answers. The surest way to make a mess of marriage; or go into frustrate a friendship; the surest way to alienate a child, is to go into that relationship where a decision needs to be made with ready-made answers.

Now the third thing. The crisis comes in our lives when those ready-made answers won't work anymore. And the decision-making becomes a crisis, leaving many people feeling powerless and others bitter and resentful. For some people, a crisis becomes an obstacle, and they're bitter for the rest of their lives. They'll either go through life saying, "If only, if only, if only." Or, if you allow them, they'll tell you what might have been if it hadn't been for that crisis.

But there's another way to face that day when a difficult decision needs to be made. And that is to go through that journey and come out of it with a better quality of life. So, what's the difference? Isn't it true that a crisis becomes creative when we're willing, for a while, to live in the neutral zone?

For three years after his conversion, Paul, then known as Saul, lived in a neutral zone, developing a life of caring and compassion for others. He had to live for a while with no answers. The ready-made ones wouldn't work anymore. But living in a neutral zone made him teachable. He became humble, and he became receptive to the grace of God.

I had a client in my counseling practice battling the demons of addictions—prescription drugs, and alcohol, to mention only a few. He was also a very domineering and opinionated man. He decided he needed to go on a weeklong retreat for persons battling sobriety. He said, "When I returned from that retreat, my heart had changed."

But as I observed his behavior, he had become nothing more than a domineering, opinionated recovery fanatic. His heart and his behavior remained strangers. He wasn't willing to stop and take some time to live in the land of in-between. Neutral: When you stop going down the rabbit hole of self-destruction and haven't yet understood how to go another way.

But how? What do you have to do? You don't know. You humbly admit that you don't have any answers because all the solutions you've used before don't work anymore. People who come to me for counseling often live in that land of in-between. They are ready to become patient and teachable. They are willing to live their lives without answers. It is in the counseling environment where people feel safe to discover the best way to go, which can take what seems to be a lifetime. Counseling can be painful because the therapist won't be handing out a packet of answers. But they will give you the confidence to live without answers in this land of in between. It is only then, when we are willing to live without any pat or ready-made answers, that we can let the great solution take hold. And what is that answer? That we are accepted just the way we are, warts and all, where, by faith and not by solutions, we wait for the one who is the hope of all our years.

A colleague of mine, now deceased, lost his young daughter to leukemia. His colleagues urged him to get back into the fight and model that this tragedy did not defeat him. But he refused. He said to me, "First of all, I don't want people to think that my loss did not turn me upside down, and many who have been through this agree. Secondly, I did not want to 'short-circuit' this grief as if it hadn't affected my life. I needed to feel this grief deep in my soul and see what changes it would make. I owed that to my daughter."[4]

To live without answers is painful. To live in the land of in-between, the land of neutral, is like going through the shadows of the Twenty-Third Psalm. But it is in that land where we must wait for the one who is the hope of all our years by faith and not by answers or spiritual laws.

Kathryn Koob, in her book *Guest of a Revolution*, describes the 444 days she was held hostage and blindfolded in the US Embassy when the Iranians captured it. It's also where I found the title for this lesson.

Rather than being bitter about the crisis she was caught in, she said, "I would go beyond where I was with love and see that I could learn about my spiritual life during that period when I was living in a neutral zone."

"Looking back," she said, "I learned about the meaning of joy during those days more than all the years I had before that."

Every day, she prayed the same prayer that communicates that it's OK to live without ready-made answers when in a crisis. She prayed this prayer: "O God, keep my heart and soul open to receive you as you are and not as I imagine you to be!"[5] If you have one or more days when you find yourself in the neutral zone … don't lose patience with yourself, and be open to that grace that will never let you go.

Suggested scripture: Galatians 1:11–24

Questions for Journaling and Conversation

1. Can you give examples of ready-made answers?
2. Were any of them helpful in your relationships?
3. Can you recall ever being in a "neutral zone"?

Hope is a state of mind, not of the world.

Hope, in the deep and powerful sense,

is not the same as joy that things are going well,

or willingness to invest in enterprises

that are obviously heading for success,

but rather an ability to work on something

because it is good.

—Valav Havel

CHAPTER NINE

Days When…
You Want to Take Revenge

Have you ever been so mad at someone who hurt you that you could hardly wait to get even? That you enjoyed planning your revenge. As we examine this human emotion, I urge you to journal your thoughts and feelings.

In this lesson, we ask what you do when you're so mad, so angry, and hurt that deep within you is this desire for revenge. Where do you go for help? I have found that I need to take it one step at a time.

Dr. Lawrence Kohlberg of Harvard carefully studied moral development in children.[6] Out of that study, he developed six moral development levels that humans can but may not go through.

For a few moments, I want you to focus your mind on someone you like or want to get even with. As I review these six levels, on this day, what level are you on?

Level number one. "Something is wrong only if you get caught." The scandal of sexual harassment being exposed lately is clearly on this level. But we learn as children that obedience and punishment go hand in hand.

Tragically, many adults translate this level into defining their relationship with God. When tragic things happen, whether it be a tornado or cancer, it is a punishment by God.

Obey or be punished. We learn this as children, but it will not help us on those days we want revenge.

Second level. Something is suitable if it feels good. But our feelings will not help us when we want revenge because it tastes so good. Jesus focused his message on our will, not our feelings. A feud never has to continue if you turn to your will and say, "I'm going to decide to stop this grudge right now!" And let it die. You don't have to have the last word. You don't have to strike the final blow.

The third level of moral development. We decide what is right by whether or not it pleases other people. While we may desperately want to have the support of others, it will hardly help us on the day we want revenge. We can always find someone who will be pleased when we take revenge. They will nourish our hurt and justify our retaliation. They will tell us how we are right to do so. But this level will not be helpful on revenge day.

The fourth level is where we have a sense of duty toward a set of rules. This is the level of law and order, commandments, creeds, principles, policies, rules, and regulations. It's the level that holds our society to be civil. However, the problem with this level is that policy is often placed ahead of humanity.

The fifth level decides between right and wrong by the most significant amount of good it does for the greatest number of people. At this level, a person realizes it is possible to do something legal and still be wrong. This is a level in which one may hear whispered, "Thou art not far from the Kingdom!"

And now the sixth level. This is where the saints reside. It is the level at which we can say, "What does the greatest concept of God I know require of me in this decision? What does God's love demand on this day I desire revenge?"

On that day of revenge, this is the level where we ask, "What will be redeemed? What will be redemptive in the life of the other person? What will change the direction in which this evil is going?"

What level are you on your journey? When it comes to revenge, what level do you seek? Wherever you are on your journey, revenge may not be as important as deciding to take that next step. We may hear the peace that passes all understanding in our hearts, "Thou are not far. Not far at all."

Once we learn the levels of recovery, then we can examine our revenge more honestly. First, we must accept that vengeance has roots in all of us. There will be no healing without first honesty. To confront ourselves and admit that unlike in school, where the three "R's" are reading, writing, and arithmetic, the three Rs are revenge, resentment, and retaliation.

Secondly, revenge can be exhausting. And the cause of it cannot be found in our bodies or minds. Someone once said to me, "Revenge is mind-exhausting. It's what wakes you up at two in the morning. It's what causes us to lose our temper. It's what pushes us to be abusive to ourselves and others. We build walls around us to protect ourselves from being hurt any further, but these walls also prevent someone from loving us.

Thirdly, the one word that can sabotage the healing process is the word "justification." Justification keeps us focused on what the other person did to us. This person was close to us. Someone we had entrusted ourselves to them. The only thing that will enable us to focus on what's going on in ourselves is what we call forgiveness.

The power of forgiveness is not what it does for the other person but for what it does to you. Forgiveness says, *"I'm going to put that garbage down and not poison my life with it any longer."* The stress and strain can then begin to heal.

And fourthly. If we are ever to overcome a day when we want to take revenge, we must be sure who our ultimate audience is. We may blurt out, "I'll show him or her!" as if that person is the maximum audience. We need to say, "I'll show God." This then frees us from playing with each other.

This anecdote. I was in a stationery store to buy a get-well card for someone in the hospital I had trusted, and that trust had been betrayed. I selected one that had the Old English print with the very pious statement on the front: *"God loves you."* And then, on the inside, it said, *"And what's good enough for God is good enough for me."*

That's the spirit of our scripture. Feed our adversaries by reaching out to care and to forgive.

Suggested Scripture: Romans 12:9-21

Questions for Journaling and Conversation

1. "Don't get mad; get even." What happens to us when we adopt that path as a solution?
2. When is it time to forgive? Is there a right and wrong time?

CHAPTER TEN

Days When…
You Feel Like You've Been
in a Wrestling Match

Jacob was left alone, and a man wrestled with him until daybreak. When the man saw that he did not prevail against Jacob, he struck him on the hip socket, and Jacob's hip was put out of joint as he wrestled with him. Then he said, "Let me go, for the day is breaking." But Jacob said, "I will not let you go unless you bless me." So he said to him, "What is your name?" And he said, "Jacob." Then the man said, "You shall no longer be called Jacob, but Israel, for you have striven with God and humans and prevailed. (Gen. 32:24–28)

The scripture for this teachable moment refers to the time when Jacob was heavy into deceit with his uncle Laban, his brother, Esau, and perhaps even God. There comes a moment of intervention for Jacob when he wrestles with an angel or perhaps the gift of God within himself. But at the end of this "wrestling," Jacob finally finds out who God calls him to be. Only then is Jacob's name, "the crafty one," changed to Israel, which means "the trusted one."

Jacob's pilgrimage is a journey that all of us have to take. We all have days when we will wrestle with deceit and cynicism and hopefully move to a spirit of faith and trust, not only with God but also with our family, friends, and ourselves. This shift to faith and trust requires risk. But therein lies our state of mental health and a "barometer" for our relationships. It calls for us to exercise our free will, which is symptomatic of wellness and wholeness.

What tools are needed when we are in a wrestling match like Jacob? The following four questions could be empowering. The first question is, "How important is it to trust others?"

"Trust none," said Shakespeare, "for men's oaths are like straw, and their faiths are like wafer cakes," which are very thin. A Slavic proverb says, "Trust none but yourself and your horse." And if you've had any horseback-riding experience, you would know to be cautious about the horse. A Hebrew proverb says, "Never trust a man who will tell you all of his troubles but none of his joys," which is worth pondering.

And we say, "I wouldn't trust him within a ten-foot pole" and "I wouldn't trust him any further than I could throw him."

Should we trust other people? We don't have a choice. We trust people all the time. We get in the car and drive to the store. We trust drivers coming the other way will stay on their side of the road. We'll go to a restaurant. How do you know that the chef feeding so many people will not decide to spice up your meal with a portion of his saliva?

You have to trust. We trust surgeons and nurses and pharmacists and teachers with our children.

Indeed, the very fabric of our society is held together by the trust we deposit in each other. We could not survive without it. Thus, the answer to the question "Should we trust other people?" is self-explanatory. We do it all the time whether we like it or not.

Come, then, to the second question about trust. "How much should we trust other people?" Many would answer, "I'll trust other people, but no more than I have to." And why is that the most popular answer? Because so many of us have suffered the consequences of trusting someone who deceived us.

A woman in counseling cried out, "I'll never trust another man as long as I live! I've been taken for the last time!" There are similar chants of husband to a wife, a child to a parent, a parent to a child, and a best friend to a best friend. A betrayal of trust is always an inside job. You have to be a friend, a confidant, a relative, or a family member before you can be in a position to betray. We don't let our enemies close enough to betray our trust.

A third question: What happens to the human spirit when it whittles trust down to the least possible extent? What happens to the soul of the person who is always controlled by suspicion and guided by mistrust?

I had had a very emotionally draining day. I went home, only to know I had to go out again that evening. When I came home, all I wanted was to be left alone. I sat in the living room and wrapped the newspaper around me like a curtain, symbolizing

"Don't mess with me."

Suddenly, I felt someone tap my shoe. I looked over my curtain, and there was my seven-year-old son. "Daddy, can I take off your shoes for you?" I said that would be fine, and then I disappeared behind my paper curtain.

Then, there was a touch on my shoulder. I looked over my curtain, and it was my son again. "Daddy, can I get you a glass of water?"

Now, I had been a father long enough to be suspicious. What was he buttering me up for, and what did he want? What I didn't wish to do at this moment was to debate with him about what he couldn't have. I suggested he let me be alone for a while, and I returned to my paper curtain.

The next time I became aware of my son … somehow, he had been able to crawl up on my lap, put his head on my shoulder, and fall asleep. His hair had become damp against his forehead from the warm day. It wasn't a halo I was looking at, but he looked as angelic as any angel I could imagine.

I suddenly realized that my son wasn't trying to get something from me, but he was trying to give something to me. I had missed a precious gift because I was so suspicious. There's something funny about curtains, about walls. They keep people from hurting us and prevent them from loving us.

45

The last question: Is trust a gift or a reward? Those who say reward will say, "I will trust you whenever you prove to me that you are worthy of my trust." But that isn't trust. It's controlling. It's manipulation. And in counseling, people discover that isn't a good foundation for any healthy relationship. But John's God, John's Jesus, says trust is a gift. Grace is a gift. And, as a gift, it can change, redeem, restore, and renew.

One last story: There's that powerful scene of Huckleberry Finn and the runaway slave, Jim, going down the river on a raft. And Jim begins to talk.

> Every time I hear the water on the side of the river go, "Ker slap," it reminds me of my little daughter, Elizabeth, and how I treated her. She was but five years old, and she had the Scarlet Fever, and she's had a powerful rough spell.
>
> One day, I entered the room, and she was standing in front of an open door. And I said, "Lizabeth, shut that door." And she just stood there, smilin' at me. And I said, "Lands sake, chile, did you hear me? You shut that door!" And she just stood there smilin' up at me.
>
> Oh, Huck, I was mad! I went for that chil' and slapped her on the side of the face that sent her a-flyin'! I went into the other room and was gone for about ten minutes. When I came back, that child was standing there, her head down and tears running down her cheeks, and she was moanin', but the door was still open.
>
> I was mad, Huck. I went for that child when all of a sudden, it was the kind of door that swung inner, and all of a sudden, the wind blew the door shut ... BANG! She didn't even move. I crept behind her, put my mouth down behind her ear, and shouted as loud as I could, "HEY!" She didn't even budge.
>
> I picked her up into my arms and cried, "O God, please forgive ol' Jim, 'cuz he ain't goin' to forgive himself

as long as he lives!" She was just plain deaf from the fever. And here I had been treating her so.[7]

Has that ever happened to you? We get more information and cry, "O God, if I had only known!"

When we regard trust as a reward, with our children, for example, we demand consistency, performance, and guarantees from them. But John's Jesus said, "God doesn't ask for guarantees or performance. God's love is a gift, as my son's love was a gift."

That changes our lives. It changes our relationships. It makes us better together.

Questions for Journaling and Conversation

1. Are faith and trust the same?
2. Can one stand alone without the other?
3. Have you ever been in a wrestling match, literally or figuratively?

CHAPTER ELEVEN:
Days When…
You Are Fed Up With Yourself

As a psychotherapist in private practice and a clinical investigator for a large health insurance company, I was on planes regularly, usually business class. It was not unusual to be sitting next to someone who was also flying because of their work.

On one flight, I was seated beside a well-dressed businessman who apparently waited for the plane to depart in the airport cocktail lounge. When he discovered I was a psychotherapist, he said, "I think I need to talk to you." And then he poured out his pain. He told about his failures in marriage, all three of them. He talked about the conflicts at work with his colleagues, how he had let his children down, and what he had done that he wished he hadn't done.

After two hours of intense conversation, two more drinks, and the anonymity of being on an airplane, he put his hand on my arm, had drunken tears in his eyes, and said, "You don't know how much I hate myself." With that, he grabbed his briefcase and walked off the plane.

We never saw each other again. But I will always remember his parting words, "You don't know how much I hate myself!" Because he's not the only one who has touched that level of mental and spiritual illness. There may be someone reading this who can remember being at or near that pain level.

Imagine for this teachable moment that Zacchaeus was such a person—a hated tax collector, an exploiter of his people, and hated by everyone; a man filled with feelings of failure, fear, and hopelessness. This was where Zacchaeus was when he met this man, Jesus. I wouldn't diagnose Zacchaeus with a mental or emotional illness but with "emotional littleness."

> He entered Jericho and was passing through it. A man was there named Zacchaeus; he was a chief tax collector and was rich. He was trying to see who Jesus was, but on account of the crowd he could not because he was short in stature. So he ran ahead and climbed a sycamore tree to see him, because he was going to pass that way. When Jesus came to the place, he looked up and said to him, "Zacchaeus, hurry and come down; for I must stay at your house today. So he hurried down and was happy to welcome him. All who saw it began to grumble and said, "He has gone to be the guest of one who is a sinner. Zacchaeus stood there and said to the Lord, "Look, half of my possessions, Lord, I will give to the poor; and if I have defrauded anyone of anything, I will pay back four times as much. Then Jesus said to him, "Today salvation has come to this house, because he too is a son of Abraham, for the Son of Man came to seek out and save the lost." (Luke 19:1–10)

This emotional littleness must not be dismissed. It is a tough time in someone's life. Psychiatrist Abraham Maslow wrote of a student who understood this pain and self-worthlessness and went out to the city dump and, just before he shot himself, cried, "This is all I'm worth!"[8]

No, we are no strangers to how Zacchaeus may have felt about himself that day when Jesus called him out. And yet he compensated for these feelings of insignificance and unimportance by being a tax collector, feared and powerful. He occupied a position of exploitation and intimidation. He had everything except the one thing he needed. When he realized this, Zacchaeus decided to change his life. But how much change can a person make?

The late William James, a Harvard professor who ordinarily was an optimistic man, once said, "By the time a man is thirty years old, his character will harden like plaster, and he'll never be able to soften it again."[9]

Do you believe that? How much can we change? We know that people can change when they hurt enough when they get tired of the direction they're going in, when there's no longer any satisfaction out of what they're doing, and it's painful, and they get fed up with that pain.

Change and attitude are closely linked. The most essential, spiritually drained, threw their arms around each other, laughed, and wept simultaneously. Part of the change is discovering and believing that you can change.

When Zacchaeus climbed up in that tree, for once in his life, he thought less about what other people thought of him and more of what he thought about himself, and that's the beginning of change. He couldn't explain it. Foolish? Yes. Undignified. To be sure. But this man from Nazareth might have hope for him. He didn't care anymore about how people perceived him. He didn't want to spend another day hating himself like the man on the plane.

Jesus sees Zacchaeus, calmly walks over to him, and begins a conversation. "Zacchaeus, come down." My interpretation of those three words? "Come down from the pressures you've put on other people. Come down from loving things and using people. Come down, Zacchaeus. and let's have dinner together."

How long they talked, we don't know. But I can imagine that they talked all through the night. Zacchaeus was a hurting man, as was the man on the plane. Both would need more than a fifty-minute hour. But somewhere in this encounter, I imagine Zacchaeus finally standing up and saying, "Lord, you don't know how much I hate myself!" for, in the final analysis, the approval Zacchaeus sought wasn't his to give. God has written in the very souls of our lives the gift of His support; the only way we can get it is by receiving it.

Then Jesus said, "Zacchaeus, you are the light of the world! You are a child of God." Then Christ addressed Zacchaeus's mental distress, the most precious gift a person can give to another: his self-respect, his sense of self-worth.

Dawn broke, and the two men, physically, emotionally, and spiritually drained, threw their arms around each other, laughed, and wept simultaneously. And Jesus said, "Today, Zacchaeus, salvation has come to this house."

God grant that someone reading this, feeling insignificant and putting themselves down day after day, may hear the Master say, "Come on down. Come down from loving things and using people. Accept that you are already loved and understood and forgiven and accepted. That God's grace surrounds you and will restore you. That you are free. You are free indeed."

Questions for Journaling or Conversation

1. What ways do you use to hide from this grace?
2. Is the tree a possible metaphor?
3. Who can you trust?

CHAPTER TWELVE:

Days When...
We Need Care-Fronting

Read Ephesians 4:1-7, 15

The adult Sunday morning class called Conversations meets once a week, and our purpose is to grow together spiritually. But John and Charles Wesley, the founders of Methodism, brought small groups together once a week, like Conversations, and they were asked four questions. Are you ready?

1. What known sins have you committed since our last meeting?
2. What temptations have you met with? How were you delivered from these temptations?
3. What have you thought, said, or done of which you doubt whether it is a sin or not?

These questions, while direct and perhaps even uncomfortable, were designed to foster genuine self-examination and mutual spiritual growth. The Wesleyans believed that real transformation required honest conversation, not just with God, but with one another. Their approach emphasized vulnerability and trust, creating a space where members could support each other in their journeys of faith.

4. Have you nothing you desire to keep secret?

Does anyone like to be held accountable to a group and follow that format? It gets even better. If you wanted to be a part of a small Wesleyan group, listen to the questions you had to answer before you would be admitted.

1. Do you desire to be told your faults?
2. Do you desire that every one of us should tell you from time to time whatsoever is in his heart concerning you?
3. Do you desire we should tell you whatsoever we hear concerning you?
4. Do you desire that in doing this, we should come as close as possible?
5. That we should cut to the quick and search your heart to the bottom?
6. Is it your desire and design to be, on this and all other occasions, entirely open to speak everything that is in your heart without exceptions, disguise, and reserve?[10]

Does anyone wish we go back to the good old days? Is anyone ready to stand and sing "Give Me That Old Time Religion?" Paul says, "Speak the truth in love." Is that possible? And, if it's possible, is it desirable?

There are five points to this teachable moment. First, we don't like to be confronted. I used to say, "If you have something critical about me, talk about it behind my back but don't bring it to me face-to-face."

"Confrontation." We have a confrontation with a neighbor. And then there are those "therapeutic" confrontations. Someone we cared about was sick or addicted, and people who "cared" about them would fight with them so they would get help. But often, these confrontations failed because there was so much hostility. Jesus did not say before it makes you free, it should first make you feel miserable. We don't like being confronted.

The reason why we don't like confrontations is that they are usually filled with demands and ultimatums. You expect an "appropriate" apology, or you expect someone's behavior to be modified. Confrontations rarely succeed in getting either.

Paul discovered why you couldn't demand from another person the very thing you most want, and if you and I could get a hold of that and not let it go, we would save ourselves a lot of misery, heartache, and divisiveness.

And that's the third thing, and it's even a key to recovery. Paul discovered that God had given no one power over another person's inner life or spirit.

You remember that story of a mother who, in the act of punishment, put her son in a corner, and her parting words were, "You are going to sit there all day or until you change your attitude!"

But her son's parting words to his mother were, "You can make me sit here all day, but inside I'm standing up!"

That's the glory of being an individual in God's sight. God hasn't given anyone power over your inner spirit, and you don't have power over anyone else's inner spirit, either. And I would suggest that even God has given up control over our inner life, our spirit. God wants our love, but we must be free to give it.

This leads us to the tricky question: Does this mean that we can never speak the truth to someone? You have a friend or loved one whose behavior or addiction is slowly killing them, undoubtedly killing their career and relationships. Can you speak the truth to them—to say to them, "You're making a mistake!" Will they listen or find all kinds of reasons not to believe you? And good reasons. Does it mean that we can't speak the truth to one another?

Paul says to the people of Ephesus, and he wants us to overhear it. "You're leaving off the last two words: 'Speak the truth in love.'"

That leads to the last thing. No one cares about what you know until they know you care. This raises the question of how we relate to people we have conflict. If you can, think of a person with whom you have conflict. You have five options. First, you can say, "I'll get even with them! I'm going to win, and they'll lose, and for me to be right, they have to be wrong, and they are!" That's the way many people deal with conflict and controversy.

The second way is to say, "OK, I'll get out. Since we can't agree and you're not going to change, I don't fit in anymore, so I'll leave." And that's the way many people handle a confrontation. The third option is not to fight or flee but to submit and give in. "I don't like confrontations, and I don't like this struggle, so I'll give in. You can have your way." Submissive on the outside and bitter on the inside.

A fourth option is "I'll meet you halfway" or "Let's compromise." People (usually politicians) get a lot done through compromise. It's the way of coping, but it's not the way of rejoicing. This leads to the fifth option, the one that Paul spoke about. And that is, "I care, and I'm going to confront." "I care and want this relationship to continue, but I want it to continue honestly and with integrity, and I need to tell you what's happening to me inside."

David Augsburger calls this *care-fronting*. It's a two-edged sword. Caring that doesn't have moments of confrontation is irresponsible, and the relationship will most likely deteriorate and die. The other edge of that sword is that conflict without genuine caring will come across as cruel, and the relationship will not survive.[11]

How do we put the two together? Two words: grace and judgment. Care-fronting. God does this to us all the time. God repeatedly says, "I will confront you, but I will hold on to you with a love that will not let you go!"

Can we do that? Can we? Dare we do anything less with one another?

Questions for Journaling or Conversation

1. Briefly describe how you confront a problematic relationship.
2. What has been your response to a failed attempt at care-fronting?
3. What do you need to learn and apply the next time you need to care-front?

CHAPTER THIRTEEN

Days When…
The Solution is the Problem

While on a flight to Atlanta, I was seated next to a young woman who lived in Atlanta. As soon as we were airborne, she began to converse with me. She seemed pretty upset, and after some polite courtesies, she asked me the inevitable question, "What do you do?"

I am always hesitant about what to say. If I say that I'm a therapist and counselor, they will either stop talking or start talking and get a free hour of therapy. I have never been able to come up with an alternative answer except for the truth. But I've tried. I once said, "I'm a brain surgeon, and I'm on my way to an important case." To the other extreme, "I do nothing, and this is my busy season!"

When I told her I was a psychotherapist in private practice, she said, "Oh, well, I need to talk to you!" And that is when I should have said, "No problem, I charge $170 per hour." But I didn't, and she began with, "All my life is filled with problems, problems, problems!" And for the rest of the flight, I think I heard about them. But the one that seemed to be bothering her the most was that she had broken the heel of her shoe and didn't know how she would get home with it. Don't worry, I was nice.

Life is problems, problems, problems. Life often feels that way. The ice cream falls off the cone; the melon isn't ripe when you open it; there's a cricket in the kitchen.

Sometimes, it's worse than that. Because of unemployment, the rent is going to be late. Again.

Sometimes, it gets worse than that. One of your children needs immediate dental care, and your credit card is maxed out.

Sometimes, it gets worse than that. The company is cutting back on personnel, and your boss comes over to you and says, "I need to talk to you for a minute in my office."

Sometimes, it gets worse than that. Your child wakes up in the middle of the night with a temperature of 104, and you have no health insurance.

Sometimes, it gets worse than that. The lab results just returned, and the biopsy was diagnosed as "malignant."

Sometimes, it gets worse than that. An elderly parent that you had promised several times to visit but you never got around to it, died before your visit was made.

Life is like that: problems, problems, problems. To be human is to know issues. And as this woman flying next to me needed reminding that if your fundamental goal in life is to have a problem-free life, having been born was a real mistake.

These are a few things to add to the fire. First, humans indeed put a premium on learning how to cope. I have a colleague on the East Coast. He was one of a handful of therapists in the US who specialized in building a practice around children diagnosed with life-threatening illnesses. We would all meet once a year and support each other for the many losses we had come to endure.

My colleague and I talked often, but the conversations were brief. He was dying of lung cancer. When I asked him how he was doing, he said with great difficulty, "I'm surviving. I'm just trying to cope with today."

We put a premium on learning how to cope. It's a tremendous skill to have in a crisis. I am convinced that learning how to cope is an excellent tool, but it shouldn't be the only tool because there must be more to life than survival and coping. Making coping the most crucial goal will make us restless because coping is living with a problem without a solution. Is there something more than just managing and surviving a problem?

> Someone in the crowd said to him, "Teacher, tell my brother to divide the family inheritance with me." But he said to him, "Friend, who set me to be a judge or arbitrator over you?" And he said to them, "Take care! Be on your guard against all kinds of greed, for one's life does not consist in the abundance of possessions. Then he told them a parable. The land of a rich man produced abundantly. And he thought to himself, "What should I do, for I have no place to store my crops? Then," he said, "I will do this, I will pull down my barns and build larger ones. And there I will store all my grains and my goods. And I will say to my soul, 'Soul, you will have ample goods laid up for many years; relax, eat, drink, be merry.'" But God said to him, "You fool! This very night your life is being demanded of you. And the things you have prepared, whose will they be? So it is with those who store up treasures for themselves but are not rich toward God. (Luke 12:13–21)

In this scripture reading, a man says to Jesus, "I have a problem and a solution …" And Jesus listens to this man's problems and his solution and sees that his solution is his problem. The man says, "If you could persuade my brother to divide his inheritance more equitably, everything will be all right."

In Jesus's pre-pandemic story, the farmer's primary goal in life is security. When his crops were ready for harvest, they were better than expected. Problem: more than his barns could handle. Solution: "I will tear down my barns and build bigger ones, and then I can relax with all that security." And God said to this farmer, "You fool! Tonight, your very soul is required. What good are all those barns to you now?"

Sometimes, we think that security and being in control is the solution when, in fact, that solution is the problem—learning to cope with our current situation. There's more to life than just learning how to cope.

What to do? Jesus possessed what we pursue. Jesus consciously claimed and carefully nourished such an intimate relationship with God that the power, energy, strength, and spirit continually flowed in and through His life. It's what the New Testament called the Holy Spirit. And it's what prayer is to us. "Prayer? You're a counselor, and that's your solution to my problem?"

"No. But it is a way to give you time to bring the same power Jesus used to discover the right solution." Unfortunately, we have relegated prayer to ritual: "Our Father, who art in heaven." Or for protection: "O God, watch over me and mine." Or grocery list prayer: "O Lord, hear my prayer," and then read off your list. No, that's not the kind of prayer I'm suggesting.

What I am suggesting calls for you to get a new attitude. To be still for more than thirty seconds. Be still, and let God begin to flow in and through you. And how do we acquire that kind of power, that level of prayer?

First, you have to be more receptive. Or, more importantly, some of us need to learn to be still. Once we have learned to be still, we must remind ourselves that we are alive because God willed us to live, to pray, "In God, I live and move and have my being. In God, I live and move. In God, I live. In God."

Then, we are ready to focus on the kind of God Jesus revealed.

And what does that God look like?

In Seattle, a bridge crosses over to get to downtown, and underneath, three hundred feet below, are industrial buildings. This bridge has no deterrents to prevent people from climbing over the side and jumping to their deaths.

One morning, I was crossing that bridge when I saw a young man climb over the railing, and it was clear he planned to jump. I stopped my car right in the middle of traffic, and, despite horns blaring behind me, I walked over to the man, who was now on the other side of the railing.

I looked over the railing and said, "My name is Bill. What's yours?"

"James. But go away. I need to do this."

"You mean, splatter yourself all over the rooftops down below? Is that what you mean?" And I then climbed over the rail and stood next to him. Carefully.

"What are you doing? Don't get close to me. I'm going to do this, so stay away!"

As he is saying this, people in their cars are irate, and many are yelling, "Jump! Jump! You're making me late for work! Jump!"

"James, I climbed over the railing because I want you to know that whatever possessed you to do this, you need to know that you are no longer alone. Whatever possessed you to want to kill yourself now has me on this side of the bridge, and I'm not going to let you jump."

I slowly reached over, grabbed the back of James's shirt, and said to him, "I know that if you jump, holding on to your shirt won't prevent you from falling. But, James, if you jump, you will probably take me with you. Is that what you want to have to happen?"

That broke James's resistance, and tears came to his eyes. He then allowed the firefighters who had arrived to bring him back gently and slowly to the other side of the railing and safety, and a life was saved.

That's the kind of God Jesus revealed. It isn't blasphemy to say that the God Jesus told each of us, "If you go, then I will be going with you."

We are not saved by creeds, beliefs, formulas, doctrines, or even our good works. We are saved, whether in or out of the church, by only one thing: the love of God and our response to it. When we collaborate with the God that Jesus revealed, we discover a released power to do more than cope, overcome, and move on.

Questions for Journaling or Conversations

1. How do you strive for more security?
2. In the story of the parable of the farmer, what was the message he was implying?

Hope is a waking dream.

—Aristotle

CHAPTER FOURTEEN

Days When…
You Do Not Know About Tomorrow

Something familiar in this post-COVID age is that we don't know about tomorrow. Martin Luther cried, "What's more miserable than uncertainty?"[12]

Poet and philosopher Soren Kierkegaard insisted that uncertainty is the source of anxiety. He said, "Anxiety is the next day."[13]

Anxiety is not knowing. Anxiety is living in the middle of a deadly virus. This element of uncertainty surrounds us. If we go beyond coping and get what he suggests from James's scripture, then let's examine these five available steps.

People try to cope with anxiety and uncertainty by gathering as many guarantees as possible. At every age, men and women have longed and looked and struggled and searched for someplace or relationship where they could feel secure and protected against uncertainty and the problems that come with uncertainty.

For example, some people think that if they get married, their problems and stress will be solved. "If I could find the right man (woman), all my problems would be solved." Others believe that if they acquire as much money as possible in their "portfolio," they will have no problems. Still, others seek some form of guarantee via carrot juice and exercise. One such person became my client, and at his funeral, I overheard someone say, "My! He doesn't look well." Indeed. And then there's this belief that if they could find the right place to live, with the right schools, house, and neighborhood, all their problems would be solved. People try to cope with the uncertainties in life by acquiring more guarantees than can be obtained.

Another way we try to cope with uncertainty is to try to live for tomorrow. We put our energy into working and planning for a great future, and, finally, everything will be under control. And what does that look like? All the bills will be paid, the children will be out of the house and happy with life, and all of our problems will be solved. Then we can relax at last and enjoy life. Even Jesus said a person with a "tomorrow lifestyle" is a fool.

Still, others will find solace in lamenting the past. People begin each day by parking their lives where they judge they were happiest in the past and want that to happen again—to live in an illusion.

The Letter of James, however, suggests another way—a fourth way. James says that the only way to make peace with the uncertainty of tomorrow is to regard and receive, affirm and accept each day as a gift. He states that it is an act of arrogance to believe tomorrow is a given. Only today has been created. The arrogance that tomorrow is guaranteed is the life of a fool.

That leads to the last alternative. This scripture is not saying, "Live for the moment." That is escapism. This scripture is not saying that we shouldn't plan for the future. But do this without the arrogance that tomorrow is guaranteed and thus be careless about today. And we let anger, resentment, and grudges go on and on, convinced that tomorrow is already ours.

But the ministry of the uncertainty of tomorrow is to energize our confidence that today is a gift and this is the day that the Lord has made. And, thus, do that reconciling, that forgiving and loving, not just to others but also to ourselves.

This last thought: I came across a book by L. M. Goodman entitled *Death and the Creative Life*. Dr. Goodman interviewed famous artists and scientists, such as Alan Arkin, Isaac Stern, and Nobel Peace Prize winners.

The number of questions she asked them about death and dying was this question: "Do you think that if it were possible that we could do away with death, would it be a good thing?"[14]

Death is not some monkey wrench that God has thrown into the machinery of life but a purposeful part of God's providence. Knowing that this day is a gift, that tomorrow is not yet given or guaranteed, energizes us to live fully now.

Questions for Journaling or Conversations

1. How has this pandemic virus changed your attitude about tomorrow?
2. It is suggested in this teachable moment five ways to cope with anxiety. Is there one that works best for you?
3. Is there anything you can't let go of in your past?
4. How would you answer Dr. Goodman's question, and why?

CHAPTER FIFTEEN

Days When…
To Really Say Forever

The primary purpose of this teachable moment is to discover how we can deal with the stress and strain that come from our intimate relationships. That could include a spouse, a child, a parent, or a close friend. How can we care for those meaningful relationships in such a way as to nurture them and give new life to them?

In this scripture, Jesus is trying to describe that kind of relationship, which can be read using metaphors. The people listening to him knew about vines, branches, vinedressers, fruit, and pruning, and he said, "That'll do." He would use these terms as metaphors to describe this intimacy in our relationship with God. And remember pruning a plant is not punishment but prepares the plant for a more productive life.

> I am the true vine, and my Father is the vine grower. He removes every branch in me that bears no fruit. Every branch that bears fruit, he prunes to make it bear more fruit. You have already been cleansed by the word that I have spoken to you. Abide in me as I abide in you. Just as the branch cannot bear fruit by itself unless it abides in the vines, neither fan you unless you abide in me. I am the true vine, you are the branches. Those who abide in me and I in them bear much fruit, because apart from me you can do nothing. Whoever does not abide in me is

thrown away like a branch and withers; such branches are gathered, thrown into the fire and burned. If you abide in me, and my words abide in you, ask for whatever you wish and it will be done for you. (John 15:1–7)

As a therapist, I have discovered at least five stages significant relationships can go through. Unfortunately, some relationships get stuck in one of these stages. However, there is the hope that knowing there is another potential stage in the future often helps that relationship get unstuck. As we go through the rest of this lesson, imagine a relationship you feel challenged with and what stage you are on in that relationship and what it would take to move to the next step. The first stage is the stage of enchantment. At the enchantment stage, we make many promises that we seldom carry through. It is in the enchantment stage where we say to the other person what I call "forever statements." "We are so much alike." "You are the one I have always wanted to spend my life with."

Enchantment. It's also what drew the first disciple to Jesus. Biblically, this is the stage of grace. We feel loved and accepted without having to earn it, where we say, "You accept me just as I am. You don't put me down. You encourage me." Grace.

But what we thought was the "forever" stage is not, and we fall out of that stage and into the second stage. The stage of disenchantment. The stage of disappointment: "You let me down." "You didn't fulfill my expectations." And when the disciples got into this disenchantment state, the scriptures say, "They all fled and ran away."

This is also the accusation stage: "You never listen to me!" "You don't talk to me." "You don't respect my feelings." This is also the stage where relationships, especially marriage relationships, get involved in those power struggles: Who will run the relationship? Who's going to have the last say? Power struggles. Not compassion but competitiveness. The location of disenchantment.

Some relationships get stuck in this stage for years. If we do, we will take the route of the disciples and run away. But if we decide not to run away and instead ask, "What can I learn from this?" that's when God pulls us to that third stage. And that's the stage of acceptance. This is not the stage where we are loving or caring. This is where we learned some things in our disenchantment stage. We learned some insights. The question now is whether we will accept these insights. Hopefully, we learned that we couldn't control or change another person by an act of will. Not only must we know that, but we must also accept it.

Second, in the disenchantment stage, we learned that love could not be demanded.

Third, we learned that we could survive. In all intimate relationships, there is pain, disappointment, and death. But we will survive. Now, can we accept it? In my counseling practice, I witnessed several individuals and couples who survived this stage and then came to know something of the power God had given them. They came to know more than they'd ever known before—that they could hurt, but they also could heal.

This leads us to the fourth stage, the commitment stage. Commitment means choice. It means, "I must choose this and not that. I can't go through life living in between." Commitment means that I give up the "if onlys." "If only I would stop being so critical." "If only she would stop feeling so much self-pity." Commitment means getting off blaming one another. Commitment means taking responsibility for that relationship. Commitment means letting go of believing you will win a power struggle and stay in that relationship. If you stay in a relationship, and it's going to be intimate and forever, one can't win, and the other one loses. Power struggles don't work.

Commitment means letting go of having to save face and defend our egos. Commitment means letting go of the desperate hunger for security. Some of us are so afraid that we will end up abandoned that we cling to security. A truly intimate relationship needs to let go of the security blanket and live by faith and trust together.

Commitment means getting rid of those resentments and past hurts and getting in touch with the power of compassion and forgiveness. We are forgiving the other person and ourselves for our faults, our cowardly behavior, and our selfish choices and beginnings—again and again.

Then we can journey to the fifth stage, which is the great stage Jesus is pointing to, and that's the stage of co-creation. A woman went to her doctor complaining about her problem. He listened patiently. Finally, he took out his prescription pad and ordered the following medication: "Go to the Grand Canyon." She said, "How will this help me? I've got a serious problem!" And he said, "I want you to see something bigger than your problem."

We are all well-connected. At this stage, we hear God say, "I will be with you always." We as a church need to get to that level—to be cocreators and begin to see that we're in the relationship for the whole world and are here to bear one another's burdens. That's commitment. And how do we do that? By listening, giving a genuine hug, holding, forgiving, and by a note that reads, "Thinking of you."

A mother became concerned when her nine-year-old daughter came into the house from the playground ten minutes later than allowed. She said in her defense, "I saw Mary sitting on a bench and crying because she had just broken her doll." "Oh," said her mom, "and you stopped to help her fix it?" "Oh, no, Mommy. I stopped to help her cry."

We can carry our burdens alone when we must if we have been willing enough to share them when we can. I don't know which stage you're stuck on, but maybe you need to let loose of self-pity. You may need an encouraging word from God: "Listen, there's something beyond you. Get engaged in the suffering and the hurts of others, and you will find something to be grateful for. That will be the day we can say, 'Forever.'"

Suggested scripture: John 15:1–7

Questions for Journaling and Conversation

1. What stage can you best describe when you think of a difficult relationship?
2. Who do you recall was there to help you gel through that time?
3. What gives you passion? What gives you purpose and meaning?

CHAPTER SIXTEEN:

Days When…
You Are Breaking And Need Patience

Patience isn't considered a spectacular virtue until you need it and don't have it. Someone has said the only difference between a coward and a hero is about five minutes. Maybe that applies to patience as well. It was just being able to hold on a little longer after everyone else had given up.

How many relationships have come to an end … How many relationships never even began … or reasonable goals have never been achieved … how many feelings never happened because someone who could have made the difference came to the end of their rope, threw up their hands, and said, "I'm through!" And then, of course, there's the Patient Prayer: "Lord, give me patience, and I need it right now!"

So, where do you get it? We get a glimpse of it in the scripture lesson. The setting is the final week of Jesus's life, a horrible week. Everything caved in. Jesus was in the midst of the last meal with disciples that he had hoped he could depend upon but would also abandon him. Knowing all this, he takes the bread, breaks it, and says, "Each time you eat bread, I want you to remember that I will never give up on you."

Patience. When you are breaking, where do we go to get the patience we need?

We quickly learn that patience is not acquired by going out after it. People who make it a mission to develop patience always miss it and seldom are very patient. Some of the most impatient people I know are the ones who are always telling me how hard they work to be patient. At best, they manage to be tolerant, and there's a world of difference between being kind and patient.

You ask any child. The children I worked with were frequent flyers in children's wards. And they would often evaluate staff who tolerated them and those who were patient with them. They know the difference.

I like the story about the husband, who was concerned about his wife's health. She had lost all her enthusiasm. She had lost all her energy. There was no sparkle in her eye. He took her to doctor after doctor because they couldn't find out what was wrong with her.

He took her to an old doctor who was also a wise counselor. He sat behind his desk and listened to this woman tell her story, and, suddenly, he got up from behind his desk and went over to her and kissed her on the right cheek and then kissed her on the left cheek and went back and sat down. And, like a miracle, the sparkle returned to her eyes, the color in her cheeks returned, and she was like a new person!

The doctor turned to her husband and said, "Well, that ought to do it." And the husband said, "I don't understand!" And the doctor said, "My prescription is that this woman needs to be kissed twice a week." And the husband said, "I still don't understand, but if you think that'll work, I'll bring her in every Tuesday and Thursday."

Well, he missed the point. And you and I continually miss the moment when you and I can get patience by simply going out after it, pursuing it, or pouncing on it. We'll never get it that way. Patience is a by-product—by going out after something else, and you find patience the world will neither give you nor take away. It's a by-product.

Not only is patience a by-product but it's a by-product of being involved in doing something you believe is worth doing, whether you fail or not. We are usually most impatient when we are doing something that is not worth doing.

Jesus never once said to anyone, "Seek ye after patience." He knew it was a by-product. He said, "Seek ye first the Kingdom." Get involved in something worth dying for or living for, and patience will be added unto you.

I had been retained to prepare a community for the death of a person revered by all. It was a small town, and its civic leaders would experience grief. I would spend two weeks conducting several small groups focusing on loss and how they would cope with the death of someone they all revered. It was a monster of an assignment, and it would conclude with a community meeting in the high school auditorium.

I was sitting in the local coffee shop having breakfast, and a gentleman came in a wheelchair. He had quadriplegia and was accompanied by a gentleman, his primary caregiver, and a chauffeur. His van outside was huge. When their breakfast came, his manservant would cut up his food and place it on a special mechanically powered fork he would use to eat. He saw me watching him, smiled, and asked if I would care to join them.

We spent the next three hours in that restaurant, getting to know each other and telling stories that would describe our lives.

We would spend the next two days discussing our lives, careers, and community.

He was a very successful businessman in the exploration of natural gas. Thirteen years before our encounter, when he was forty years old, he anxiously awaited news of a significant natural gas discovery. He said, "I had so much nervous energy and no patience waiting out the time. It was in that time when I was in a horrible accident that would change my life forever."

He would go from being a long-distance runner and avid skier to being a quadriplegic. I asked him, "How do you go from running marathons and looking for places to dig for natural gas to using a wheelchair?"

"Bill, I had it all, but I had nothing. My life was all about me. How much money could I make? How many sports competitions could I enter? I had no patience for anyone who got in my way of winning. And then it all changed. I was in massive depression and wishing I could find a way to end my life. But as time passed, I learned three things had to happen. The first thing I had to do was adjust. The second thing I had to do was adjust. And the third thing I did was adjust. I went from a me-centered lifestyle and athlete to a spiritual athlete and community leader."

I would learn that he was the one who had retained my services, and he would eventually join me at the community meeting, and together we would talk about looking outward and how to care for others. He said, "I became a man with patience with not just myself but also my staff and family and now the small church I pastor. I have found purpose and meaning that I never had before."

Patience when you yourself are breaking.

A postscript: he would die from complications of pneumonia soon after our encounter. I often wonder if he was preparing the community for his death as well.

Suggested scripture: Matthew 26:26–35

Questions for Journaling and Conversation

1. My benefactor found the gift of patience as a by-product of a terrible accident. Can you recall what happened when you discovered patience?
2. Was there anyone in your life that gave you the strength to get through that time?
3. What gives you passion? What gives you purpose and meaning?

CHAPTER SEVENTEEN

Days When...
You Can't Let Go

This was more than twenty years ago. It was late, and the storm was relentless. As I turned in to go to bed, I thought of how relieved I felt that I didn't have to be anywhere that night. As I crawled into bed, I heard someone pounding on my front door repeatedly, and the person seemed to be calling my name. I was home alone, and all the lights were out. I got up, put on my bathrobe, and went to the door. I turned on the porch light and yelled through the front door, "Who is it? Who's out there?"

A moaning, sobbing voice responded as the person continued pounding on the door. "Please, please let me in. I can't live like this any longer! Please!"

I opened the door, and in fell this older woman, soaked from the rain; her hair was disheveled and dripping from the storm. She was shivering from the cold, wet, sobbing through it all and unable to make sense of her situation. But she was able to introduce herself as we walked into the front room, and I asked Jeanne to sit down.

I turned on the heat, lit a fire, and started the coffee. I sensed that this was going to be a long night. Then I suggested she go in and shower and get in some dry clothes I had selected that I thought she could wear. I said, "Jeanne, I insist that you do these few things, or I won't be able to help you. But if you shower and change, this will give you a few moments to breathe and calm yourself so we can discuss this. Otherwise, I need to call 911." Thirty minutes later, Jeanne returned to the living room, sat, and stared at the floor. There was a slight improvement in her state of mind.

"Why did you come here, Jeanne, and how did you find me?"

She said, "I heard you give a lecture about your work with the terminally ill. And you're in the phone book. Dr. Stephenson, I need your help. Ever since my husband died, I haven't been able to function. I can't live like this any longer. You've got to help me. You've got to!"

I never see clients in my home and rarely see adults without children in a life-threatening crisis, but saying no to someone in distress at midnight didn't seem like a good idea.

"Jeanne, tell me your story."

"Just before my husband died, we had a terrible argument. Before we went to bed, I screamed at him, 'I wish you were dead!' The next morning, I woke up, and next to me was my dead husband."

She said, "I am responsible for my husband's death. It's my fault. This guilt has burdened me. I was too distraught to go to the funeral. I often never get out of bed. I don't know how to live alone. I cry constantly. I rarely venture out of the house. I've stopped seeing my friends or attending church because I keep crying. Even my children have grown weary of me and don't want my grandchildren around me. My world has ended, and I want to die."

We can all understand how people like Jeanne can become vulnerable to decisions that could be painful to overcome. Is there any hope of healing the Jeanne's in this world?

The author of the Gospel of John told the story of Lazarus to proclaim to everyone who thinks that they've made a total mess of their lives that we can come out of those tombs and recover. For some, it's a lousy job. Suppose you hold on to it because of the uncertainty of the economy; better to hold on to it. The misery of the present is better than the insecurity of the future. That job guarantees food and a roof over your head for you and yours. Or maybe it's the tomb of resentment you keep holding on to. Letting go of it couldn't lessen the pain and hurt, and you don't want to.

Before Jeanne left my home that night, I asked, "Jeanne, I failed to ask you when your husband died?"

She paused briefly and said, "Eleven years ago, but it seems like only yesterday."

Lazarus's story is ours for two reasons: First, Jesus's power enables us to bury the past. Note that Jesus let his friend Lazarus die. This doesn't make any sense. But he does. Even Mary and Martha are bewildered by this. "Lazarus would still be alive if you had just come on time. Why didn't you come sooner?" Jesus could have kept Lazarus from dying, but he chose to let Lazarus die and then bring him back in resurrection.

This is a story of the resurrection, not resuscitation. This is a story of new life, not raising the old. But the senior needs to die; it requires a tomb. The old relationship needs to die so a new one can be born. People like Jeanne, we need to have a Lazarus moment—to let the old die so that a new life can be taken.

But some people like Jeanne won't let the old die. They keep holding on to it. They can't let go of the misery they are in. They are frozen in the present even though time keeps moving on. And then they become bitter, resentful, and vulnerable to making poor decisions, or the depression becomes so overwhelming that they would rather be dead than alive.

Our lives are in phases: From childhood to adolescence to adulthood to middle age to old age, from being single to being married to being single again to being married. We go from being parents of children to being parents of adults to being parented by our children. We go from working our tails off to wishing we could retire to retiring and wondering what we will do with all this free time.

But we must let one phase die so a new one can live—to trust that God will give us the gift of new life. Grace is what we do with that new life. Meaning and purpose are found when we discover that we can accept and embrace the new life God has given us.

Second, can we trust that God will give us new life if we let the old life let go? Isn't that the crux of the matter? If we were on a trapeze swing and the catcher was on the other, would we have the faith to let go of the swing, turn, and be caught by the catcher without knowing if the catcher would be there? But first, we have to let go.

I had a client, just twenty-three, and battling leukemia. She was in the hospital because she was out of remission and losing blood. Suddenly, she gasped, lost consciousness, and began hemorrhaging. They rushed her into surgery to stop the bleeding, but the monitors were flat-lined. Miraculously, the surgery would give her another chance.

She recalled that episode to me. She said, "Five doctors were standing over me. Each one of them worked feverishly to keep me from dying. I knew I was indeed very near death."

Then she said she began to pray. We must all say this prayer when we have to let go of the old, not knowing what the new life will be like. She prayed, "God, I let go, and I turn my life all over to you now. I am letting go and turn it all over to you."

That's a Lazarus story. It's what we must all do, perhaps more than once if we are to receive new life from the one who gave us life in the first place. If we ever hope to experience a new life or a new way, we must be ready to pray, "I turn my life all over to you. I let go." And as you let go, you turn to be caught.

Even Jesus would swing without a net. And as He let go, he said, "Father, into Thy hands, I commit My life." Not only are we embracing God as our creator, but God is also our re-creator again and again and again …

If you are ever part of a conversation and hear someone say, "My world is in such a mess, I just want to die." We are all given the power to say to that person as we stand outside whatever tomb they are in, "Come out. Whatever it is that is keeping you from really knowing life again, let it go and come out of your tomb." But be ready. You may have to say it more than once. Some people are hard at hearing.

Suggested scripture: John 11:17–44

Questions for Journaling or Conversation

1. Is there a loss you can't yet find peace? Describe the conflict you have with this loss.
2. What is it that keeps you wanting to grieve?
3. What will it take for you, like Lazarus, to come out of your tomb?

CHAPTER EIGHTEEN:

Days When...
No One Seems to Care

For the writer of the book of Acts, the fundamental meaning of the Holy Spirit is Power. "And you shall receive power from on high. And they spoke the word with power. And with great power, the apostles gave their witness."

In the passage for this teachable moment, the evidence of that power is given briefly. "And with great power, the apostles gave their witness and grace was upon them, and there was not a needy person among them." There are only two ways to achieve that kind of qualification: that kind of church membership. One way to do it is to be very selective in your membership, like a country club. To become a church member, your income and wealth must be at a certain standard. The other way to do it is to take care very seriously—to have such a mechanism in the church that the church responds in ways appropriate to every person's need to care for everyone.

But care is a muscular word, a harsh word. It's not just standing around in a pool of pity or sympathy, feeling sorry for the world's condition or each other. So, what does it mean to care? Two stories.

My father had an interesting relationship with the church of which he wasn't a member. But if anything needed fixing ... he was there. If a widow needed something fixed, he was there with his toolbox. The pastor was constantly giving him calls to get something repaired. And even though he wasn't a member, we gave generously. But get him to come to church? He saw the church filled with a bunch of hypocrites—people who say they care about others but are looking after themselves. He had no patience with people who saw the church as a one-hour-a-week event. He would say, "They are careless, and they care even less."

The pastor visited us, and my dad let him have it. My father said to him, "The church doesn't care about me. The church just wants what I can give and my pledge. The church only comes around when they want something from me. Isn't that the real reason you are here?" he said to the pastor. I used to hear him say that again and again.

One time, he didn't say it. I was sixteen, and he died of a rare disease in Jamestown General Hospital. I came to see him and say goodbye. I had been his primary caregiver for the last two years. We were very close. He was now just a shell of the man I adored. He was deathly weak and in an oxygen tent. I looked around the room: potted plants and cut flowers on all the windowsills, a stack of cards twenty inches deep beside his bed, another bouquet.

Every card, every plant, and every blossom were from persons or groups in the church! He saw me reading the cards. He then whispered to me a quote from Shakespeare, which I often read to him, "In this harsh world, draw your breath in pain to tell my story."

"What is your story, Dad?"

And he whispered, "I was wrong."

While director of a counseling practice I had named Counseling Associates for Seattle, my colleagues and I volunteered our services at a hospice for people with AIDS, it was at epidemic proportions, and the facility saw a high death rate and few good deaths.

The people I worked closely with also attended my adult Sunday school class at a local church. At least a dozen others in the class were members of the church. It was a class where one could speak the truth, which was, on occasion, painful to share and also sad to hear. I knew my colleagues and I were reaching a place of emotional exhaustion. We had lost eight clients in one week. We were all wearing our emotions on our sleeves. But in this class, all the gloves could be taken off, and the truth could be brutal.

On that particular Sunday following the deaths of eight of our clients, we were discussing in the class the difference between a caregiver and a caretaker. And that's when one of my colleagues, a social worker named Sally, broke down, not in tears but in anger.

"That's it. I'm hanging it up." She was a social worker and had just finished working with an AIDS patient we had all come to love and cherish.

"Sally, do you need a break? Take some time away from this work."

She said, "No, I'm quitting."

"You're quitting?" I said.

"I'm quitting."

"Why are you quitting?"

"Because nobody cares."

"Oh, c'mon. There isn't a person who works with us who doesn't care."

"Well, you're deluding yourself. Our team is filled with a bunch of ego-centered, highly ambitious, get-all-you-can-as-fast-as-you-can people. And I'm quitting the church too. They're the pinnacle of not caring. Talk about hypocrites! They come in their Sunday clothes pretending to care, and then Monday comes, and 'Get out of my way!'

"I have yet to meet anyone in this church who cares. I would be nothing more than a stranger if I didn't wear a name tag. Nobody cares."

"Sally, you're wrong. I come to this church and teach in this church because the people here care more than any other church I know. They have learned to take care of each other. The stranger is safe here."

"Oh? If you're so sure of that, name some committed to caring. Go ahead, Bill, name some!"

I knew that no name I gave would work for her that day. She was in a state of "compassion fatigue." Sally did quit, but, like my father, she would eventually say, "I was wrong."

Suggested scripture: Acts 4:32–35

Questions for Journaling and Conversation

1. Recall and share a time when you made a terrible decision. How did it make you feel?
2. Do you recall feeling so overwhelmed that you didn't think you would ever get past it?
3. Who helped you become "liberated" from that tomb? What did they say or do that helped turn things around?
4. Have you ever witnessed a "Lazarean moment"? Who do you know could use one?

Learn from yesterday, live for today, hope for tomorrow.
The important thing is not to stop questioning.

—Albert Einstein

CHAPTER NINETEEN:
Days When…
Praying Seems a Waste of Time

A young man, a husband and father, came to me for counseling. Doctors told them their daughter was not developing as she should. There was some trouble with her hip joint. They took her to a surgeon and discovered that major surgery was needed, and there was the possibility that she would never walk again.

As the day of surgery drew nearer, the anxiety for him and his wife became nearly intolerable.

In a session, this young man said to me, "I can't pray. Every prayer sticks in my throat. I am so filled with anxiety and apprehension. Even the Lord's Prayer doesn't work. My anxiety is becoming anger, and I did as you requested; I began to write in my journal." He pulled out his journal, and this is what he had written:

> Our Father, who art in heaven. Why aren't You down here
> on earth doing something about my daughter? Who cares
> if Your name is hallowed or whether or not Your kingdom
> comes, when what concerns me most is my daughter's
> welfare …

He was bitter and cynical. He was also very scared of the unknown. I asked him to take a moment and breathe, and then I asked him to write to his soul and focus on his daughter. With tears in his eyes, he wrote about all the joy his daughter had brought into his life. Even if she would never walk again, she had already been an incredible blessing and would continue to be.

He began to realize that he was focusing on what he didn't have rather than what he did have. After sharing this with me, he returned to his journal, and, with the creative and poetic gifts he had, he wrote these words:

> Our Father, despite the present difficulty, you are still in heaven, and the world is still ordered. May my response hallow Your name. The coming of Your kingdom is more important than this present difficulty, so may we not hinder its appearance with worry and anxiety.
>
> Cause this event to be an opening up in me to Your will and a new way. I must recognize that You still provide the necessities of life. We have bread enough.
>
> May this event help me to realize how important it is to be in a good place with those I love, to secure Your forgiveness and forgive those who have sinned against me. May this not be an occasion for temptation, to lose faith.
>
> Deliver me from any evil response or action in this difficulty. Life's overriding and all-important fact is that the kingdom, power, and glory belong to You forever. And this event is caught up in that fact. Amen.

As a writer, therapist, and layperson, I will be careful not to tell more than I know when it comes to prayer. The best I can do is to be as honest as possible about my journey with prayer. Hopefully, you might find some parallels with your journey. I have reached out to the one person in my life whose life with prayer has been a model for those days when we have judged that praying on that day is just a waste of time.

As a child, I used prayer as a form of protection. "Now I lay me down to sleep …" I never missed it because I was afraid of not waking up the following day! Prayer was a form of duty, a guilt trip, a form of protection. And I included all my family and friends in the prayer of protection. I called this the "All State" prayer. I was in good hands so long as I didn't forget to pray.

As I got older, my prayer life required that I give God a job description. I wanted God to be good to me and mine, just as I tried to get acceptance in my relationships. Like I was trying to earn approval and kindness from others, so also with God.

A woman I counseled had a boyfriend who went into the Navy and was on board a ship for nearly a year overseas. While he was gone, she dated his friend, and they became more than friends. But their affair didn't last, and when her boyfriend returned, they picked up their relationship, which finally issued into engagement and marriage.

One year after their wedding, she finally confessed her experience with this other man in a moment of intimacy. He responded in anger. He was hurt, and he became resentful. He never let her forget it. She said, "Ever since then, I spent the last twenty years trying to earn his forgiveness."

Perhaps some of you know what that's like. So often, we have to earn people's kindness and beg them for mercy and acceptance. And many people translate that kind of human experience into their relationship with God. They feel they have to woo and beg God to be good to them and theirs. They have to earn God's forgiveness through their works and by praying and begging.

But this concept of prayer began to collide with my work with the terminally ill and a new understanding of my relationship with Christ. In my private practice, I wanted so badly to succeed. I would pray before each session that God would make this a good session and that the client/family would walk away from it better prepared to face the future.

And then I had an "Aha!" moment. I suddenly realized that God wanted more for my clients than I did. As if God was saying, "Pray for them, yes, but also pray that you stay focused. And sharpen your skills because, Mister, you will need them for this client." I didn't need to give God a job description. I should listen to the one God has for me.

From this realization, I soon learned the discipline of prayer as collaboration. Some time ago, I was counseling a man whose wife had died, and I was active in her care for the last few months of her life. But now, a year later, he was considering remarrying, and our sessions were often about his struggle. In one of his last sessions, I asked him, "Sam, what did you learn about human relationships from your first marriage?"

He replied, "I was always testing my wife, whether she loved me enough. And I would remain silent. I wouldn't tell her what I needed or wanted. Believing that if she loved me, she would know this. If I should marry again, and now I'm going to, that God has not given us the power to read each other's minds and that to test another person's ability to read our silence an infantile way to relate to those around us. I need to express my needs and wants openly and trust that the other person will respond."

That's collaboration. It's infantile to demand that our loved ones read our silence. Now, translate that over to our relationship with God. Why do we have to ask God for anything? Doesn't God already know what we need? Yet Jesus used words in prayer such as "seek," "ask," and "knock." Not because God doesn't know but because it empowers us to learn more honestly and clearly. Then, God can collaborate with us. We can then let go of what we wish to control and be more receptive to God's love and will. But it takes collaboration.

When it comes to prayer, what stage or level are you on? Whether you feel boxed in or don't see the value of taking time to pray, I want to offer up this prayer on our behalf. It's just you, the reader, and me, the writer. This prayer I share with you.

> O God, each of us must examine how we resist Your will—ways we're going in the other direction, rituals in which we're worshiping our wants rather than following Your will. Hear now, O God, in this moment of quiet, as we each offer our spirit to You in a new way and collaborate with Your choice. (Pause)
>
> Perhaps someone reading this knows that a different decision must be made. A turnaround needs to be made in their lives and how they make decisions. A different spirit must be brought up to collaborate with Your will, which is our peace. Hear that person now, O God, in this moment of quiet. (Pause)

O God, we go now knowing that to believe in You is to think that the future is always open. To believe in You is to believe that all the rules will be fair. To believe in You is to know that our life is filled with good surprises. Amen.

Questions for Journaling and Conversation

1. What is the purpose of prayer for you?
2. What adjustments do you need to make prayer more relevant for you?

CHAPTER TWENTY:
Days When…
Hope Depends on You

There are times when all hope is lost. We get caught up in dwelling on the past or consumed by a present with little promise of change. When that happens to those you care about, it may require you to carry that hope for them, and, in some cases, you may be the one who will restore their hope.

Being the "custodian" of someone's hope calls for particular skills. For example, it calls for a determination not to let failure and frustration have the last word. It calls for someone in their life who has a "never-ending" hope. Someone who has lost all hope will need people who can remind them of hope and will never abandon them even when they feel all hope is gone.

But to have that belief requires special skills. The first one is this. We need to remember that we exist before we are complete. We are human becomings. We are all unfinished business.

In my practice, I had a young boy and his mother, and I asked to prepare them for some very aggressive therapy to address his rare form of cancer. This would begin with extracting bone marrow from his spine, which was a complicated and excruciating procedure.

We tried everything to reduce his anxiety and fear. We even attempted through hypnosis to give him a "glory spot" where the procedure would be done in his lower back and spine but to no success. Now tied down, his mother holding his head, and just before they placed this very long needle into the bone of his spine, he cried out, "Oh, Mommy, I wish that God had not made me!" Now carrying hope for both of them, his mother said to her son tearfully, "Oh, my darling. God has not yet made you. God is still making you, and right now, it is painful!"

The other essential skill to have when hope depends on us is to remember that hope calls for more than just believing it but also applying it. Hope and grace follow the same path. To receive the gift of grace calls for this grace to be gracious. To obtain the gift of hope calls for us to be disciples of that hope. The following story was shared with me. But the source could not be found. I don't even know if it happened. But the message it carries happens all the time.

Ellen and Brett had become a very well-respected and successful couple. Still in their twenties, they had grand plans, which included a wedding of all weddings. But then came the auto accident, leaving Brett in a deep coma with extensive head injuries.

After hours of lifesaving procedures, Brett was pronounced dead. However, just as they were about to move his body to the morgue, one doctor decided to check for pulse one last time and discovered a very faint one.

Brett would remain in a deep coma for more than three months. His mother and Ellen were told several times that Brett had only a few hours to live. Both refused to accept that prognosis, and they dug in to face the long haul of his recovery. Everyone else had given up any hope for Brett.

Ellen's hope had a purpose. She was at his bedside every night, talking to him like it was just another day. She would begin the "conversation" with "Hi, Brett, how was your day?" Then, she would talk to him as if it was just a typical day and share what went on in her day.

Ellen's hope for Brett would not be shaken. As she left the hospital each time, she offered a prayer that had become her "mantra": "The Lord is my shepherd …"

One day, Brett opened his eyes. He couldn't speak or move, and no one knew if he could comprehend anything. But Ellen remained hopeful.

Brett's progress was slow and painful. Movement returned with a finger, then a hand, and so on. His speech went from guttural sounds to mumbling to a slow and careful response. But progress was happening. Eventually, Brett was discharged to home to continue his physical recovery with Ellen as his daily physical therapist.

It would be a full year of hard work and painful rehabilitation, but Brett would have his speech restored to the point of going to Ellen's father and mother to get permission to ask Ellen to marry him.

He would also walk again, and on their wedding day, Brett, with his walker, walked down the church aisle. He then turned and, standing painfully upright, watched as Ellen was escorted down the aisle with her father.

As she came down the aisle and toward a life of devotion to Brett, she got Brett's attention and winked at him. He couldn't yet wink, but with a smile, he blinked his eyes and smiled. As she neared the altar where Brett was waiting, she whispered, "The Lord is our shepherd …" It was a wedding filled with victory, love, and unconquered hope There are times when we may be called upon to carry the hope for not just ourselves but others until they can also embrace that hope.

Suggested scripture: Isaiah 43:1–5

Questions for Journaling and Conversation

1. Take a moment and think about a current or past relationship where the "storm clouds" block any chance for hope to shine through.
2. Despite the pain this relationship brought you, did the brokenness teach you to be more sensitive and thoughtful of others?

It is of hope that you suffer.

It is through hope that you'll change things.

—Maxine Legace

CHAPTER TWENTY-ONE:

Days When…
All Hope Seems Gone

O ccasionally, I will have that experience where I know I have just visited the kingdom of God. Several years ago, I was facilitating a small group of men and women who were all dying of AIDS. Twice a week, they would meet to share their "story" with this horrible disease. They often called themselves lepers because they only had fellow lepers to relate to. Everyone else had excluded them.

One early, stormy evening, as we sat in a circle together, there was a silence in the room. The only sound was the pounding of the rain against the windows. We didn't even have the lights on. The atmosphere represented the spirit of hopelessness and alienation that many in the group felt.

Then, the eldest person in the group, a Jewish man in his late seventies, said, "I brought with me to the group this bread that a family member just made. It's still warm, and it tastes so good. I want to share it with all of you."

We passed the bread around the circle, each taking a healthy slice and putting soft butter on the slices that he had also brought. We all waited until everyone had a slice of bread. He blessed the bread, and we began to eat as the rain continued to pound against the windows.

Moments later, we realized the rain had stopped. We looked out, and the clouds were breaking up. The most beautiful sunset replaced the storm, and a rainbow began to take shape. We stood up and put our arms around each other, and, shoulder to shoulder, we looked out the window as the sun began to set and a rainbow poured into our meeting room. In that moment, the bread we shared, the storm and then the rainbow, the unconditional trust we had in each other—all this instilled a special kind of hope in each of us. A divine hope. An eternal hope.

They all died within weeks of each other, but in that circle, we each got a taste of the eternal kingdom. We each felt surrounded by a great cloud of witnesses, reassuring us that the kingdom of God was not far.

Questions for Journaling and Conversation

1. Can you recall any time when you sensed that you were not far from the kingdom?
2. Why is it that witnessing the end of a storm has so much emotion around it?

SECTION THREE:
Our Mental and Spiritual Health

INTRODUCTION

This portion of the book is dedicated to caring for our mental and spiritual health—others might say our minds and hearts. They are so closely linked together. Our behavior, what we do or don't do, and what we say or don't say will either enrich or impoverish, not one or the other, but both. I am convinced that we must intentionally pay attention to how we care for our mental and spiritual health. Excessive care is an example. This can be in alcohol consumption, prescription and over-the-counter drugs, cannabis, cocaine, hallucinogens, eating disorders, excessive exercise, to name just a few, and the one elephant in the room: Emotional outbursts.

I have chosen just a few ways we jeopardize the harmony of these two vital parts of our lives. These include ultimatums, loneliness, depression, helplessness, anxiety, and decision-making. But what indeed occurs is that our faith and mental health are undermined at the same time.

I have attempted to develop a "teachable moment" by stating and illustrating the problem and then providing some constructive "tools" to address each situation. Each "teachable moment' will attempt to offer ways to be well again, to be whole again. Where our soul and mind are in harmony again.

Neither should a ship rely on one small anchor,

nor should a life rest on single hope.

—Epictetus

CHAPTER TWENTY-TWO:

The Secret To Serenity

In *The Book of Joy*, the Dalai Lama refers to mental immunity." He says,

> "If your mental health is sound, then when disturbances come, you will have some distress but quickly recover. If your mental health is not good, minor disturbances and small problems will cause you much pain and suffering. You will have much fear and worry, sadness and despair, and anger and aggravation. The best solution to our suffering is mental immunity."[15]

That's the purpose of this series. We are addressing the issues in our live that cause mental distress and see how we can "vaccinate" our mental health so that it doesn't require a therapist, medication or even a recovery group to apply these suggestions. We continue now with serenity.

> "Not that I have already obtained this or have already reached the goal, but I press on to make it my own because Christ Jesus has made me his own. Beloved, I do not consider that I have made it my own; but this one thing I do: forgetting what lies behind and straining forward to what lies ahead, press on toward the goal for the prize of the heavenly call of God in Christ Jesus. Let those of us then who are mature be the same mind, and if you think differently about anything, this too will God reveal to you. Only let us hold fast to what we have attained." (Phil. 4:1–5).

Paul is writing this letter from prison. But I want to read you another letter from prison. This writer was a former client.

"Dear Dr. Bill. I am in prison and on death row, and I am asking if we could establish a counseling relationship through email. Thank you for your consideration, (name)."

This letter got my attention, just as Paul's letter got the attention of the Christians in Philippi. Paul is in prison, yet there is a certain freedom, a serenity, about him, and he's writing to give the people in the church the secret to his freedom and serenity. I want to share his secret for serenity and how we can care for our mental health.

As a therapist to people who often had no plans to have a therapist, I discovered the importance of being persistent with people who had given up all hope. People with a terminal illness will often separate themselves from those who are not terminally ill, who are living life when they are living and dying. But I would persist. I was determined to equip them for an "attitudinal change" and choose to live until they died—to do more than tie a knot in the rope and hang on.

There's a saying that the world will always step aside for anyone who knows where they are going. Paul learned this. He knew serenity and freedom because he was so persistent. He said, "This one thing I do …" He had determination.

The second secret is that nothing can take the place of persistence. There are as many people who are miserable, discouraged, depressed, and unhappy because of their perseverance and determination as there are who aren't. You don't know what Hell is until you've lived with someone who says, "It's my way or the highway," or "It's either my way or not at all!" These people believe that nothing can replace persistence and determination and are often the ones who think that religion is something for the weak and losers of this world. They believe the church is here to comfort the people who can't "make it" in the real world.

There's a third secret to freedom and serenity. "God helps those who help themselves" is an illusion. The Gospel says that God helps those who can't, who are powerless to help themselves. I have spent a career providing counsel to people between hospitals—the one they were born in and the one they would die in. No matter how long or short our journey is between them, the one thing we all discover is that we are helpless. And persistence and determination won't change that a bit.

Judith Viorst, in a monumental book called *Necessary Losses*, in which she tracks all of those losses that come in our lives, whether we want them to go or not, summarizes them at the end of the book. She says,

> "Somewhat wrinkled, highly vulnerable, and non-negotiable mortal, I've been examining losses: When we are confronted by the inescapable fact that our mother is going to leave us, and we will leave her, that our mother's love can never be ours alone; that what hurts us cannot always be kissed and made better; that we are essentially out here on our own; that we will have to accept in other people and ourselves the mingling of love and hate, of the good with the bad; that no matter how wise and beautiful and charming a girl may be, she still cannot grow up to marry her dad; that our anatomy and guilt constrict our options; that there are flaws in every human connection; that our status on this planet is impermanent and that we are utterly powerless to offer ourselves or those we love protection. Protection from danger and pain; from the inroad of time; from the coming of age, from the coming of death. Protection from our necessary lives."[16]

Someone told me about a television reporter who likes to ask, "If you were arrested for drunk driving and your local Sunday newspaper put the headline out, '[So-and-So] was arrested for drunk driving,' would you go to church that Sunday?"

Nearly everyone said they would not return until they had forgotten what they had done. And the reporter said, "That's ridiculous! That's like being hit by a car, and there's blood all over the place, and your bones are broken, and they send an ambulance to take you to the hospital, but you say, 'No, no! I've got to wait until I clean up this mess and I've stopped bleeding, and these bones are healed, and then take me to the hospital.'"

105

The church is for the injured, the powerless, and the wounded—for recovery, healing, and safety. If we weren't so busy hiding our shortcomings from each other, we would be amazed: "I didn't know you had been through the gauntlet, too!" The perpetual story.

That's what Paul, now an older man, finally discovered—that he wasn't afraid to die, that he had been grasped by grace, and that God does help those who can't help themselves. That's the only good news. I have personally been in the presence of more than three hundred people who died, but that has not prepared me for my own. I don't want to suffer, but I could likely suffer. I don't want to die and occasionally wonder how I'll die. Every day, I read obituaries, and Parkinson's, which I have, is nearly always mentioned. I'm not looking forward to the experience of dying. How about you? I'm not ashamed of my fear of dying, and I'm not ashamed of sharing that with you.

That's what Paul wants us to know from that prison on death row. He said, "This one thing I do ... I press on for the call of God in Christ Jesus."

When you and I discover that, whether in prison or out, we will know the secret of serenity, of the good news of the Gospel.

Questions for Journaling and Conversation

1. What can "inoculate" us with serenity versus ultimatums?
2. Why are "ultimatums" compared and contrasted with serenity? Is there something else?
3. What was the secret to Paul's serenity?
4. "The fear of sharing." Expand upon the clue as you understand it.

CHAPTER TWENTY-THREE:
On Coping With Loneliness

There are some things worse than being alone. There is the fear of being alone. That's worse. Lucy asked Charlie Brown what he would be when he grew up. "Lonely!" he answered. We need to make friends with that loneliness because it is inescapable.

This teachable moment will explore not just the pain of this wilderness we call loneliness but also what the power of being alone can give us—the value of intentionally seeking our own solitude, the wisdom, and the peace that can come from listening to our silence.

> And the Spirit immediately drove him out into the wilderness. He was in the wilderness forty days, tempted by Satan; and he was with the wild beasts, and the angels waited on him. (Mark 1:12-13)

This scripture helps us because it talks about Jesus's wilderness. The word *wilderness* appears more than three hundred times in the Bible. Whenever men and women had to make hard decisions, God led them out into the wilderness to be alone with that hard decision.

We also have our wilderness moments. These wilderness experiences can teach us two things. First, we can learn from our wilderness by intentionally listening to our lonely self instead of trying to eliminate or replace it. Popular magazines are filled with articles telling us how to eliminate our loneliness. But, if we would learn to listen to our lonely self, we might even learn to love it—to nourish it.

A man came to me for counsel. He said that his well was going dry. I asked him to tell me more, and he said he feared being alone. He had to have the TV or radio on whenever he was alone.

I asked him, "Is there any time you just spend alone?"

He said, "Alone? Oh, I'm too busy to be alone. Too busy."

The next time you begin to sink into your purple self-pity mood and feel that your inner life has dried up, you may be ignoring your lonely self. You've been neglecting it; thus, it doesn't have a word for you. Isn't it true that when we listen to our loneliness, we discover that learning how to live with others is secondary to learning how to live with ourselves? Forty days in the wilderness.

Mamie. I want to pause and paint a picture of the patient I walked in to meet. Day and night, she had an oxygen tube in her nostrils to stay alive. Her cancer was in both lungs, and she was slowly suffocating to death. The cancer was also in her bones, joints, and back. She was in constant pain even though she was heavily medicated. Every moment was agony for her.

Seldom, if ever, did anyone come to visit or offer her a word of comfort. She said, "They don't know what to say, and they can't bear watching me in such pain. This cancer has even taken away most of my body, and it's hard to even look at me. I'm not a good nomination to the church's volunteer visitors."

However, this woman's mind was as sharp as anyone I knew. Her spirit was lovelier than any flower arrangement. I sensed I was in the presence of a teacher, and my soul was about to be enriched. She invited me to sit down, and I did. I sensed that this was not going to be a courtesy call.

I sat down, and she said, "I need to talk to someone who will listen, and I believe you are the one to do that." For over an hour, Mamie would talk about her life, her family, and her faith. She told me what she was proud of and ashamed of. At the end of the hour, we were both exhausted.

As I was preparing to leave, I said, "Mamie, before I go, can I tell you a joke?" Her eyes lit up, and I told her a joke. It was funny.

Then she said, "Dr. Stephenson, can I tell you a joke?" She told it to me, and it was hilarious. We were now both laughing.

And then this silence came over us and the room. We just sat and looked at each other for the longest time. There was a moment when I felt my soul was at one with her soul. There, in that room of death, a seasoned psychotherapist and a cancer-stricken lady, both of us surrounded by the smells of disinfectant and death, giggling like two kids caught with their hands in the cookie jar. But now, it seemed like a holy moment, and that room became a sanctuary. I sensed that I was standing in the realm of God.

I leaned over and kissed her on the cheek, and she did the same. It was such a sacred moment. I wanted to remove my shoes because I knew I was standing on holy ground.

We never saw each other again. But the fear of loneliness had been overcome for both of us. Our roles of patient and therapist blended. I learned that the loneliness I was experiencing became an asset when I permitted myself to share it with someone like Mamie.

Take now the second step. In the wilderness, listening to our lonely self, taking care of that loneliness in us, somehow, we learn how to better care for others. It is one of the ironies of the way God has made us. Only as we can withdraw and be alone are we fit to be with others.

I am convinced that the cruelest form of punishment is having to eat alone. We often use it with those who can no longer participate in the community, such as a church synagogue.

In Seattle several years ago, I had been asked to provide end-of-life care for two women who were both diagnosed as being terminally ill. Both women were widows, and both of them lived alone. These women taught me to understand the power of inclusiveness and hope so that loneliness doesn't have the last word.

But Mrs. Sanderson was a teachable moment for me. She was terminally ill and, near the end, living in a skilled nursing facility. It was a beautiful place with many visitor spaces, but not one car used them. I found her room, and the staff eventually wheeled her into where I was to conduct the interview.

She belonged to a church of over a thousand members with several ministers, choirs, fellowship groups, several women's groups, bible classes, and groups that took trips.

"How long's it been since anybody from your church came to visit, Mrs. Sanderson?"

"You're the first person to visit me in over three months, and you're not even from the church." Punishment for getting sick and talking to herself: make her eat alone.

I said, "Mrs. Sanderson, may I come and share supper with you once a week? Which night would you prefer?"

She chose Tuesday, and every Tuesday for the next four months, I was there at five o'clock, waiting for her to arrive. She said, "It was so heartening to see someone waiting for me to have a meal rather than me waiting for them. Coming to this meal is something I look forward to every week, and I also thought about your suggestion and, every day, I make myself get ready to go to the dining area, and I find someone eating alone, and I go and do what you have done for me."

Hope—letting loneliness become a healthy teachable moment.

I would be going to see her regularly but always at a time when it was time to eat. It would not be long before her cancer became so overwhelming that she could not host or eat with me. But the stories. She kept repeating the times we sat together and ate together.

That was the best "therapy" I could have offered. It was amazing to see the hope come into her life, even if it were for just a few minutes. And the stories. Oh, the stories she would tell of times she had meals with her family, with her friends, and those special times with her husband, not to mention the many times she would recall when we had a meal together and the stories we shared. Hope indeed.

My alone time is when I fish. My favorite place is on this very long pier over the ocean in Ocean Beach in San Diego. In the middle of the pier is a café, and they make the best breakfast burritos. I always get one when I fish on the pier. The pier is also where many of the homeless dwell during the day. Early in the morning, several homeless will be sitting and sleeping with all their paraphernalia surrounding them. It dawned on me that I was eating my burrito alone, and they had nothing to eat. I started buying one or two more burritos to distribute to one or two persons who were homeless.

I then went a step further. I asked if we could eat our burritos together. It became known that this guy offered a burrito and asked nothing more than to have conversation. And the stories we would tell each other—to die for.

That's the secret to the Christian life. Stop looking for God. Make friends with that loneliness within you that is inescapable. Care about that lonely self within you, and you'll then care more about others. You may also discover what Mamie, Mrs. Sanderson, and the pier dwellers did—that God is in our wilderness.

Suggested scripture: Ecclesiastes 4:9–11

Questions for Journaling and Conversation

1. How do you intentionally manage your alone time?
2. How much time do you give this part of your life?
3. What obstacles do you face to do alone time?
4. If you could set a goal, how much time would you give to this part of your life?

CHAPTER TWENTY-FOUR:
What To Do With Power

I want to begin with a hypothesis. Imagine entering the sanctuary on Sunday morning and you are immediately confronted with this largely written announcement on display at the front of the sanctuary that says this:

> All of the powerful people, please sit on the right side,
> All of the weak people, please sit on the left side.

On which side of the sanctuary would you elect to sit? Some of you may have yet to decide and chose to sit in the middle of the aisle, or you turned around and left. And, of course, some would ask their wives which side they should sit on.

This picture of trying to balance power in our lives is one of the greatest struggles in our spiritual and mental health. You and I do not doubt that truth is power. But most of us need help discovering the truth about different kinds of power. And herein lies the secret to our mental and spiritual health—just two or three things.

It could help to admit that we all hunger for power. Money is power, and we go after more than we need. We do so because we will have more ability than others do.

Michael Korda wrote a frightening book loved by business tycoons titled *Power! How to Get It, How to Use It*. He says in the book that if you want to show that you've got more power, make sure that whoever comes to visit you, the chair they sit in is just a little lower than yours. He also tells you where to sit in the room and even how to dress to show others you have power. He also says to make sure they wait longer on you than when you stay when you call on them.[17]

Fame breeds power. Every year, college and professional football dominates our attention—and the commercials. Professional football players who couldn't pass bonehead English but make millions of dollars a year become the "gurus" on what shoes to wear, what shampoo to use, and how to solve the blight with drugs and gangs. Let a woman win a Miss America beauty contest, and she not only becomes an authority on facial cream but also has the answer to happiness, the homeless, and world hunger, and millions listen to her smiling answers. Fame is power.

If we are ever going to begin to put into balance the power we have, we dare not stand before God, from whom no secrets are hidden, without anything less than honesty:

"Lord, I have this tremendous appetite for power"—whether it be to the persons in our family, the people we work with, or anyone we can lord it over. But let's admit that we all have this thirst for power.

Second, the problem is not the hunger for power but the kinds of power we get hungry for. There are two kinds of power. There is internal power and external power.

What would give you more power? Answer: "Pay off all my debts." "Knowing self-defense." "Getting a higher paying job." "Never worrying about money again." This is the seeking of external power: having more possessions, more prestige, more influence. A bigger house and a Mercedes convertible.

And yet, there's an internal kind of power. Have you ever had that moment when you woke up one morning and, even though your life wasn't the way you had planned it, you were still grateful for your life? That's power.

Or, do you remember when you barely had two nickels to rub together but still felt like a million dollars? You had a powerful force inside you. This force included faith, integrity, self-esteem, self-acceptance, and congruency. You had someone who loved you, and you could love them back—internal power.

It's a spiritual power that sustains us, holds us together, and gives us the strength to recover and begin again. Internal power. It's what turns on the light and shows us the way home. I have discovered how my strengths are often an illusion, and what I judge to be my weaknesses and failures is the center of my strength.

A man came to me for counseling and poured out his painful personal problems. As he was doing so, I realized I could not keep silent any longer, and I said to him, "That's my problem, and it has been most of my life!" When I said it, I expected the man to say, "Is this what I'm paying you for? What kind of counselor are you if you have the same problem I have?"

Instead, the man, with tears welling up in his eyes, said, "You don't know how much it means to me to hear that someone like you suffers from the same problem I have, and yet you're still on top of your game."

That's what Jesus is trying to tell both the ordinary people and the Pharisees. We become faithful disciples when we see that our struggles, problems, and weaknesses have power that God can use for someone else. Without God, we cannot. Without us, God will not. Power.

For the writer of the book of Acts, the fundamental meaning of the Holy Spirit is Power. "And you shall receive power from on high. And they spoke the word with power. And with great power, the apostles gave their witness."

In the passage for this teachable moment, the evidence of that power is given briefly. "And with great power, the apostles gave their witness and grace was upon them, and there was not a needy person among them." There are only two ways to achieve that kind of qualification: that kind of church membership. One way to do it is to be very selective in your membership, like a country club. To become a church member, your income and wealth must be at a certain standard. The other way to do it is to take care very seriously—to have such a mechanism in the church that the church responds in ways appropriate to every person's need to care for everyone.

Someone is going through the loss of a relationship that you thought would never end, but it did. Hopefully, some people in their lives can come up and share, "I think I know where you are right now because I've been there as well."

Some are fighting against a life-threatening illness. Others are in deep emotional and spiritual pain because of the loss of someone they had loved so deeply. But others can say to them, "I think I know where you are right now. I've been through that gauntlet of loss and grief, and I want you to know that you are not alone." Without God, we cannot. Without us, God will not. Power.

God can use our internal strength, our scars, if you will, better than our external strength and power. We will become true disciples when we dare to share our failures, our skeletons in the closet. When we accept the truth about ourselves, warts and all, we will become a powerful message of God's grace and hope.

Suggested scripture: John 8:12–20

Questions for Journaling and Conversation

1. What do you need to give up to experience true inner power?
2. What external powers are not helpful to your life?
3. Are there powers internally and externally that can be brought into balance?

CHAPTER TWENTY-FIVE

What To Do With Depression

Depression. How do you deal with it? How do you handle your moments, hours, days, and perhaps even weeks of gloom? Is there just one way? Is there just one solution to our depression? What works for your depression may hinder someone else's battle with depression.

Writer Sam Keen said, "The key to the universe is knowing that there is no key to the universe."[18] When dealing with depression, you may get even more depressed if you adopt someone else's solution for depression. Dr. Phil does not work for some of us. What works for one may not work for another.

We can do five things when we're in the throes of depression. First, when you're depressed, remember that just because you're depressed doesn't mean you are different from other people. Whether misery loves company, you're in pretty good company when feeling miserable. There are likely others in your group who could raise their hand and acknowledge that they, too, have battled with depression. You're in pretty good company with certain key people in history, from Beethoven to Schweitzer. When depressed, try to remember that other people have gone through this kind of crisis may take some of the terror and panic away from the darkness. That's the first thing.

But that's not enough. When you're depressed, remember how to accept your depression without surrendering or resigning yourself to it. A woman who was feeling depressed went to her doctor and poured it all out, and he gave her some antidepressants. A week later, she returned to her doctor, threw the remaining pills on his desk, and said, "I don't want these anymore! They're making me feel nice toward people I don't even like!"

We need to accept depression and gloom without surrendering to it. But some people do. They surrender to the sadness and despair, and they convince themselves that the mood is inescapable and everlasting and will breed a sense of hopelessness in all your world, and that's a dangerous and potentially lethal place to be.

Do you remember the legend of the king who wanted a motto that would help in all circumstances? He assigned his wise men to the task. He told them, "I want a slogan that will help me when I'm depressed but also brief enough to have it engraved on my ring and refer to it for comfort." It was a tough assignment, but they did it, and they went to the king and presented their findings. Remember the words? Just four words: "This too shall pass."

Remind yourself that amid your emotional pain, do not surrender to it. Remember who and whose you are—that God has not written the last chapter of your book, and this too shall pass.

But that's not enough. When being depressed, we need to remember that it is not a sign of weakness to talk to another person about it. But we tend to think that. Maybe it's because we're afraid of being vulnerable and being judged.

That's when we need to listen to someone like Brené Brown when she urges us to dare greatly. That vulnerability is a sign of health and strength. Sharing your pain and depression with someone you trust or with a counselor will likely reduce the severity of that pain or depression. That's the third thing to remember when in depression.

But that's not enough. We need to remember when we are depressed, we not only share it with someone we trust or respect but also be willing to talk honestly with ourselves. We need to talk to ourselves even when others may see that as a little bizarre. But talk to yourself honestly.

As a therapist, I have learned that few people are ever really guilty about anything in the past. I have learned that most guilt has to do with the present. The chief killers of our time are not COVID, heart disease, or cancer. The principal killers of our time are the clock and the calendar. We need to look at ourselves in the mirror and ask ourselves where we are going with our lives. We need to be honest with ourselves when we're depressed.

This poem on depression was written when I was feeling overwhelmed with too many losses close together.

> As I sit here in the cold, dampness
> That is in my life,
> I realize I have lost the joy
> I had in my life
> I once had inside me …
> The hope I had in tomorrow …
> Gone.
>
> I am so completely alone.
> I need my soul to kiss me again,
> To touch me with tenderness,
> Warm and wet upon my skin,
> And whisper in my heart
>
> The claim life has upon me
> In my wider world,
> So dark and weary,
> A mystery without an answer,
>
> My thoughts reach out
> With trembling fingers
> Into the vastness before me,
> Grasping at life's more significant meaning.
>
> O soul,
> If I could just learn
> How to kiss the joy
> As it flies
> As it flies.

Self-examination can be painful and difficult. But the results can help you move to the fifth thing: depression. It's when you ask, "Where do I go?" "Whom can I turn to?" "How am I going to get through this day?"

One of the best ways of dealing with depression is to get involved in the burdens others carry. This story is a true story.

"She's a loser, is what she is!" Jack exclaimed to his wife, sitting beside him.

"This is what I was trying to tell you over the phone, Dr. Stephenson. He is constantly yelling and berating me. For no reason, he becomes very agitated and explodes. Dr. Stephenson, we have been married for over forty-five years, but since the death of our granddaughter, he has become a monster."

Jack and Marion came to me for counseling. I had agreed to see them for counseling because I was willing to see any family member of a former client for grief counseling. This one was special.

"Jack, please! Please stop it. You have no idea how deep that hurts. I lost a granddaughter, too, and you don't see me trying to take it out on you. Dr. Stephenson, life is too short, and I will not take this any longer. I'm leaving him."

There was then just silence in the room. I asked Marion if I could speak with Jack alone, and she abruptly got up and left the room, but not without Jack murmuring, "Loser!"

When she was out of the office, I remained silent, as did Jack for several minutes as he stared down at the floor and mumbled.

"Jack, what's going on? Why are you so angry?"

"Me? I'm not angry. I'm as happy as a lark, so I wonder what I'm doing here. Yes, I miss Julie, my granddaughter, but other than that, I'm doing just fine."

"Not according to Marion," I said.

"Marion. Who is Marion?"

I stared at him for several minutes as he looked around the room, the ceiling, the floor, and his watch, but never at me. I got up and asked Jack to walk with me. I escorted him to the door and asked him to sit in the lobby. I asked an associate to keep an eye on him and said, "Marion, would you come into my office for a few minutes?" She did. I sat next to her in the chair vacated by Jack. I calmly said, "Marion," she burst into tears and wept for several minutes.

"Marion, before we do any more counseling sessions, I must insist that Jack, and perhaps you, make an appointment with your primary doctor and get a thorough checkup. After that, then we can proceed. Will you agree?"

"Yes. I will call as soon as I get home."

"Better still," I said, "I want you to call right now while you have the privacy to do so."

She called and made the appointment. I asked if she would let me speak with her doctor, and she agreed. I explained to him my relationship with Jack and Marion and voiced my concern without alarming Marion. We scheduled our next appointment for a week later, and after they met with their primary doctor, Marion came alone.

"I thought it was hopeless. His abuse was intolerable. He wanders around the house swearing and talking to himself."

"But, Marion, you don't seem as tense today as last week. Why not?"

She said, "After our examinations, our doctor called me into his office, and that is when I heard the word that changed everything: Alzheimer."

"Marion, I feared it might be something like that after I spoke with Jack alone."

'The doctor doesn't think he will live more than a year. He said that Jack would need special care in less than six months. I'm losing him, but now I understand what has happened to him. He must be so confused, and you can see how frightened he is. Today, I asked him if he would tell me his name, and he just stared at me. I knew he couldn't tell me."

"But what about you, Marion? Last week, you were at your wit's end."

"But now I understand, Dr. Stephenson. My hope is in our forty-five years, which were wonderful years. I won't let this last year together be our defining moment. And I'm not alone. Our family now knows, and we are committed to giving Jack all the love we can give, and they have assured me that I won't have to do this alone."

"Dr. Stephenson, I know you only work with kids, but I need your help."

"Marion, I will be there for you, and not just until Jack dies, but I will be there for you as you struggle with his death and learn to live without him."

"I had lost all hope. Now I have a reason to get out of bed each day. I will live the vows I gave to Jack forty-five years ago. I'm going to love him whether he knows it or not."

It was a rocky time for the next few months. But then Jack stopped being so abusive, and he became more like a child and was grateful for everything being done for him. His death was peaceful, and his entire family was there as they watched Marion sitting on his bed beside him, holding his head in her arms and singing to him.

Questions for Journaling and Conversation

1. How does the poem in this lesson relate to you, and how does it speak to depression?
2. Describe what depression looks and feels like when you are experiencing it.

When you're at the end of your rope, tie a knot and hold on.

—Theodore Roosevelt

CHAPTER TWENTY-SIX

Changing Our Covenants

The Old Testament (which means covenant, by the way) has a long history of the Israelites complaining about the meaning of the covenant brought to them by Moses. The essence of that covenant is "I will be your God, and you will be My people." Said most succinctly in this one sentence, "I will be your God, and you will be My people if you keep My commandments."

They were forever questioning what that meant. What did they agree to? What was required of them? But in Jeremiah, God decides to establish a new covenant with the people of Israel. The first one was written on stone. This one in Jeremiah would be written on their hearts.

What about the covenants we make? It's the unwritten covenants we make that are the most interesting. Take marriage, for example. We know the written covenant: "For better or worse, for richer or poorer, in sickness and health." But there are many unwritten agreements/covenants of what we can or cannot expect from one another.

When my wife, Carol, had been so sick with flu and pneumonia, all she could do was sleep and cough, sleep and cough. She had a pretty rough time of it. I became the full-time caregiver, housekeeper, chief cook and bottle washer, chauffeur, laundry keeper, and even rose keeper for her thirty-eight rose bushes. I have enough thorn wounds for a crucifixion. I finally cried out, "O Lord, how long? How long, O Lord?"

Our lives are filled with unwritten covenants. Think of the ones you have in your life. And like the Israelites in Jeremiah, we must update these verbal covenants we have with each other. Do we still have the same understanding? Do we still have the exact expectations? Evaluating our covenants, especially the unwritten ones, is a healthy practice for our faith and, in many cases, our mental and emotional health.

I can appreciate why the Israelites wanted to stop updating their covenant with God. Even Jeremiah accused God of being a deceitful brook of waters that failed. But he didn't stop. He kept on going. When we come to those dry spells in our relationship with God, it's probably because we need to renegotiate our covenant with our Creator.

Is there someone you've closed the door to and refused to negotiate a new covenant in your life? To follow this God, we have made covenants; you may want to consider updating one or more of your unwritten covenants, which I call the "covenants of the heart." And maybe you will find a resurrection waiting around the corner, as near as your mailbox.

The Associated Press published an article in the *New York Times* in 1985 titled "A Drunken Fatality and Forgiveness."[19] I am grateful for their willingness to let me share it.

It's the story of an eighteen-year-old college freshman named Ted Morris, who came home for the Christmas holidays, and, while at home, he wanted to visit all his friends. And that is what Ted was doing that Christmas Eve night—driving around town, getting back in touch with his old friends from high school.

That same Christmas Eve, there was another young man, Tommy, who did not go away to college but stayed and got a job. He had been at a Christmas Eve party, and he had been drinking heavily. Tommy insisted on driving home alone, and he almost made it. Just a few blocks from his house, his car drifted across the center line, and who should have been coming in the other direction but Ted Morris, home for the holidays. Their cars collided. Ted was rushed to the hospital, but he died because of his injuries.

After they buried their son, they went to the trial when Tommy Pegage was to be sentenced because the court determined that the alcohol level in his blood was sufficient to convict him of vehicular homicide. He was sentenced to ten years in prison, but the judge gave him probation with three conditions: (1) he goes each weekend to the county jail; (2) he did not drink alcohol again; and (3) he was to periodically give talks in front of the local chapter of MADD, Mothers Against Drunk Drivers.

The Morris' were outraged! They wanted their pound of flesh. They wanted their revenge. They wanted justice. For two years, Elizabeth and Frank Morris, whose only child had been killed by this young man, closely watched and monitored the probation behavior of Tommy Pegage to see if and when he would make a mistake. They confessed that they not only wanted him to be in prison but also wanted him dead. They followed him everywhere. They made sure he checked into the jail on weekends. When he went to a party, they were always there when he came out to see whether he had been drinking. Whenever he spoke in front of MADD, they were in the audience to challenge him. After two years of monitoring his behavior, they finally caught him. They caught him with the smell of liquor on his breath, and Tommy Pegage was arrested and sent to prison to serve his ten year sentence.

Then an amazing thing began to happen to the Morris'. They thought that when Tommy Pigage was sufficiently punished and imprisoned, all their hatred and resentment would go away. But it did not. Elizabeth then did an extraordinary thing. She went to the prison and began to visit with the man who had killed her son. She said, "The hatred and bitterness I was feeling were destroying me, and I needed to forgive Tommy to save myself!" She needed to make a covenant change in her heart.

Slowly, Elizabeth and Frank began to look at Tommy in a new way. He was subsequently released into their custody and became a household member. They adopted him as if he were their son, taking the place of the one killed. Tommy became a new man, and, amazingly, the Morris' had made a covenant change of the heart, and they were released from their resentment. Together, the three of them began the journey into the realm of recovery.

Sometimes, our covenants can keep us from truly living. They can create distress to our mental health. They can question our faith. But suppose we can have the courage and confidence to update our understandings, clarify our covenants, and renegotiate our trust in others, our church, and even ourselves. In that case, God will live within and through us. And there's hope again.

Suggested scripture: Jeremiah 31:31–36

Questions for Journaling and Conversation

1. What is the difference between a contract and a covenant?
2. For example, the mortgage on your house or car loan … are those covenants or contracts?
3. What are the consequences of a failed contract? a failed covenant?
4. If you are in a permanent couple's relationship, what covenants have you made, and do you foresee them being modified over the years?
5. Your "covenant" with God?

CHAPTER TWENTY-SEVEN:

Regrets

We don't have to live very long before discovering the "might have beens": that life we nearly lived, the things we almost did, then we have to make room for regrets and disappointments. Somewhere in our lives, we will have to bring all these regrets before God and say, "This too is part of who I am." These disappointments are a part of our lives, and we must ensure they don't get short-changed.

> Beloved, I do not consider that I have made it my own; but this one thing I do; forgetting what lies behind and straining forward to what lies ahead. Press on toward the goal for the prize of the heavenly call of God in Christ Jesus. Let those of us then who are mature be of the same mind; and if you think differently about anything; this too God will reveal to you. Only let us hold fast to what we have attained. (Phil. 3:13–16)

In his letter to the Philippians, Paul talks about some of the pain in his past, his regrets, and his disappointments. For example, Paul always had ambitions to go to Spain, but he gets arrested and ends up in Rome, where he will be executed. But he says, "I forget what is behind me and do my best to reach out for what is ahead." Let's use those lines to guide us through the process.

I have several observations, and the first one is this. While we are all in this together, we're not all dealing with the same regrets and disappointments: a love that was never returned, a child who never grew to be grateful, an ambition that never became realized, a career that never got off the ground, a retirement that doesn't seem to be as exciting as planned, a relationship that can never be fully expressed, a body that doesn't seem to be getting well, the shattered dreams. We're all here in the same place but not all dealing with the same regrets and disappointments.

Second teachable moment: if we're going to be creative with these regrets and disappointments, then the way to deal with them is not to see them as a cause of our failure or to make disappointment and failure synonymous. One writer points out that the home, school, and churches are training and preparing our young people to be successful, but they are not giving them much guidance and help to handle failure.

If we are not prepared for anything but success and have no philosophy for handling failure, we are not ready to face the most ordinary issues of life. We need testimonies, not of those who have succeeded but of those who could take some disappointment and make something out of it.

Two stories were written in the *Los Angeles Times* Sports Section on the same day. The first story is about a University of Texas football player named Freddy Steinmark. After seventeen months, he finally succumbed to cancer that had invaded his whole body.

But for seventeen months, he kept that cancer from spreading to the rest of his body and continued to play football and golf on one leg. He squeezed out of the last seventeen months of his life such joy that he brought humor and courage to other people.

Toward the end, Steinmark wrote of his struggles in a book. When the publisher got the final draft, he called Freddy and said, "Freddy, I noticed that you didn't dedicate the book to anyone. Whom do you want to dedicate it to?" And Freddy, with all of that in him, all of those disappointments and broken dreams, said, "Dedicate it to the Lord. The Lord's been so good to me."[20]

On that same sports page was the story about the suicide death of Bruce Gardner, who had been a champion college baseball player at USC. He had always wanted to make it in the big leagues, but he didn't.

When they discovered his body, they found his USC diploma in Bruce's hand and, not far away, the plaque with which the NCAA coaches honored him as the champion college baseball pitcher. While we cannot unravel his motives, his friends said Bruce could never deal with his unrealized dreams.[21]

Two responses to the same kind of disappointment yet very different. We must deal with our regrets and disappointments and not make them synonymous with failure.

Instead of going to Spain, Paul ends up in prison. But rather than rolling over and saying, "This is the end, and I'm a failure," instead, we get some of the most inspiring words of the Bible out of that prison cell. Jesus took the cross, an instrument of torture, disappointment, and regret, and changed that meaning. He turned it into a symbol of human redemption.

Whatever it is you regret, your "might-have-been," the almost, the disappointment … you can change the meaning the past has for you; God has given us that power. Change the meaning of that memory, and you will be free—free at last.

Questions for Journaling and Conversation

1. What regrets did you list as you read this chapter?
2. Do you see your regrets as a sign of failure?
3. Is it possible to change them to a teachable moment?

Tragedy should be utilized as a source of strength.

No matter what sort of difficulties,

or how painful the experience is,

if we lose hope, that's our real disaster.

—Dalai Lama

CHAPTER TWENTY-EIGHT

The Sacrament Of Failure

Failure. Even when we use the capacity to forgive, that forgiveness is not always accepted by the other person, and the breach continues. Then what do we do? And here is where our mental health and our faith come together.

Near the end of Jesus's life, He began to send out His disciples to continue spreading the good news. But He knew they would face resistance, and even their lives would be at stake. He didn't want them to give up, so He said, "When they won't receive you or won't listen to you, shake the dust off your feet and go on."

That is Jesus's "sacrament" for failure; we need it as much as the disciples did. We have relationships where alienation exists, and no matter how hard we try, they aren't going to work out. Can you accept that failure and move on, or will you go on dragging that failure with you?

You may be a good father or mother, but your children may still not turn out as you hoped. Despite being a good husband or wife, your marriage will not turn out as you dreamed it would. Can you accept that failure and still go on? We need the sacrament of failure.

What does it come down to? This story. Cornelius Ryan was a war correspondent and journalist. He was the author of *A Bridge Too Far*, *The Longest Day*, and *A Private Battle*, his private account of his battle with cancer, and published posthumously by his wife, Catherine, who co-wrote the book. It is a book about, like Paul, a man summing it up. When he first hears the diagnosis, he is angry, and he writes:

I feel such a terrible sense of injustice. What did I do to deserve this? Yet that's just the question I've got to eliminate from my mind. I do not trust my ability to maintain objectivity publicly unless I can release the body quakes and shocks in private. And how can you make people who haven't got cancer understand what's happened to you without having to endure their pity as well? I don't want their pity! Self-pity is bad enough.[22]

And then, toward the end of the book, there is recorded a letter that Ryan wrote to the late Norman Cousins, his dearest friend, who was also going through a life-threatening crisis:

Bear up, old friend. In the end, loyalty and integrity to one's faith and ideals are really all that matter.[22]

The inspiration for the attitude toward failure in this teachable moment comes from this nineteenth-century disciple, and I know many of you have heard this before:

- In 1818, his mother died.
- In 1828, his sister died.
- In 1831, he opened his first business and went bankrupt.
- In 1832, he stood in the legislative elections and lost.
- In 1833, he borrowed money to open another business and again went bankrupt.
- In 1835, he met a wonderful woman. He falls in love with her, gets engaged, and she dies.
- In 1836, he entered a dark period of his life, deep depression, and was bedridden for six months. That same year he ran in the state legislative elections and lost again.
- In 1840, he presented himself as an elector and lost.
- In 1842, he met the woman he would end his life with. They marry, and she gives him four children, but three of them would die.
- In 1843, he again appeared before the legislature and lost.
- In 1845, he again appeared before the legislature and again lost.
- In 1850, his son died.

- In 1856, he ran for the Vice Presidency and didn't even get 100 votes.
- In 1858, he again ran for the Senate, and again he lost.[23]

Most people would say there goes a loser if there ever was one. Failure seemed to be his middle name. But he would echo the words of Paul, another loser: "I have completed the course, and I have kept the faith." And that may well be all that matters because 1860 he was elected president of the United States, and in 1864, he was reelected.

History would place him as one of the greatest presidents in our nation's history. But what a loser!

Failure. It is a sacrament. Failure is in our lives so we can learn from them. We don't know anything from our successes. Failure.

It is a holy time. It can be a teachable moment.

Suggested scripture: Mark 6:6–13

Questions for Journaling and Conversation

1. As a child, what role did failure play in your life?
2. How did failure apply to your relationships and career when you became an adult?
3. Can you share a failure that became a teachable moment?

CHAPTER TWENTY-NINE

Learning To Be Upset

Someone once said, "You can tell the size of a man by the size of the things that upset him." This can also apply to women. Some people get upset over the littlest of things, and some people can handle irritations that would exasperate a saint. The slightest provocation provokes some people, and they explode. Being around them is like living atop a volcano, while other people remain calm and exhibit Job's patience when in a crisis.

Could it be that God has created us so that the capacity to be irritated is the only thing that keeps us alive? And, if this capacity is necessary for our physical health, could it not equally be essential for our emotional and spiritual health?

Jesus is irritated by the money changers in the temple who put profit over people, who put their tradition over truth, who put the interpretation of scripture over helping people in need. And what we get upset about reveals what we care about. And, sometimes, we don't like that revelation in our hearts.

Have you noticed how some televangelists will often talk about who and who is not worthy of going to heaven? A two-picture cartoon says it all for me. The first picture has a man promoting Judgment Day or the Rapture, and he has his little dog in his arms. The man says to the dog, "Well, Fido, this is goodbye. The Rapture is coming, and God will take into heaven only the good and the humble. So, goodbye, Fido." In the second picture, lightning flashes, the dog is gone, and the man is still standing there. Who among us feels qualified to judge who is or isn't going to be accepted by God?

There was a workshop I was conducting for parents who had lost a child to cancer or accidental death, and one woman shared her loss of her teenage son in an auto accident. He had been quite a rebel to his parents, the school, and even the church. One of the other participants said to her, "It's too bad you will never see your son again, and he will never get to heaven because he died without accepting Jesus as his Lord and Savior." And she was crying.

We can become so obsessed with who gets to heaven that we are no earthly good. Jesus saw this about the scribes and Pharisees who turned a blind eye to poverty and hurt all around them. We need to leave heaven to God. We will trust His grace—that God loves all His children, and God has eternity to gift them with His grace.

We can be so obsessed about who is and is not getting into heaven that we become insensitive to those hurting in our world. The good news of the Gospel of Mark is that God is gracious. When we accept that grace and know that we are forgiven, we can go out into the world of our week and live like children of God.

Suggested scripture: Mark 7:1–13

Questions for Journaling and Conversation

1. Regarding the world situation, what gets you upset?
2. Regarding the national and local scene, what is it that upsets you?
3. Regarding your personal relationships, what causes you to get upset?
4. Where does God's grace fit into your reaction to all of the above?

CHAPTER THIRTY:
On Learning To Trust

I have learned that children have different ways of learning to trust. It's almost instinctual. They seem to have this innate gift of knowing whom they can or cannot trust. We adults, however, seem to have to earn a person's trust. But children's trust seems to come as a gift.

As a therapist to dying children, getting this strange man to be trusted by a child you've not known before is key to what happens between us. But once this trust is gained, it is to be on holy ground, and I was fortunate to learn about trust from these most vulnerable children.

Of all the children I had the privilege of working with, one child was the most defining example of trust. She was just twelve years old. Her name was Christal (this was not her real name). She was dying. I would be her therapist and the therapist for her mother and father for the six short weeks I came to know them.

Christal had Cystic Fibrosis, some retardation, and battled pneumonia regularly. It would kill her eventually. Initially, I spelled her name with a *y*, but she insisted on the *i*. I used to tease her about that. She would then tell me my name should be with a *v* instead of a *ph*. But I insisted on the *ph*. And then we would start thinking of other names we could play this game with. It would be our way of finding the path to the trust that would enable her to want to spend time with this "old man," as she sometimes called me.

Her parents couldn't afford the expensive medical care she needed, including a therapist. I'm not cheap, but sometimes I am free. Her parents sacrificed everything to give Christal the care they wanted for their daughter. They were amazing parents dedicated to providing their daughter with as much joy and happiness as possible. They were desperately poor but rich in their love for each other and their daughter, Christal, with an "I".

Christal's main issue was that she would never make it to thirteen, to be a teenager. She wanted the symbol a teen represented versus what a child meant. She was grieving over what could not be, not for what she was dealing with in the present.

Christal was also feeling guilty because she knew the financial bind her parents were in because of her illness. She worried that her parents would not be able to afford new oxygen tanks or breathing medicine. I convinced her doctor to "work the system" so that extra tanks would be placed in her bedroom so that she need never fear there was enough.

I urged her parents to teach Christal how to do her medications so that she could see that there was always a good supply on hand. She told her parents and me, "I'm not a kid anymore. I can do my own meds. I guess I'm a teenager after all."

One night, she asked me to come and sit with her because she could not get to sleep and was afraid she would stop breathing if she fell asleep, even though she was on oxygen 24-7. In the darkness of her room, I sat next to her bed, and we tried to breathe the same way and simultaneously. I asked her, "Christal when you are in bed alone at night, how do you slow your breathing so you can go to sleep?"

She said, "I look out my window at all the stars. I start naming them after all the people who have helped and loved me. But I always run out of stars." And we began to name the stars that night until she fell asleep. Her trust in others was unshakable. Her hope was infinite.

I had to go away for a few days. But Christal assured me she would still be here when I returned. I wasn't so confident. I called every day. She was declining and was in ICU by the time I got back.

"Hi, Chrystal with a *y*."

With great effort through her oxygen mask, she said, "Hi, Dr. Stevenson with a *v*. I waited for you."

With tears in my eyes, I said, "I love you, Christal with an "*i*.""

"I love you, Dr. Stephenson with a *ph*."

She would die later that night with her parents, grandparents, and me in the background. Early the next morning, as her parents and I were having coffee together in the hospital cafe, they said, "Dr. Stephenson, we have decided to take all the memorial money and give it to the Cystic Fibrosis Foundation, and we also plan to be speakers to support this cause. We want other parents to know they are not alone."

They were on their way. They were broke and deeply in debt, yet they had decided to place all their trust in this hope they learned from their daughter, Christal … with an "*I*".

Questions for Journaling and Conversation

1. How did you learn to trust someone? Did you learn how to trust from your parents, the church, or your peers? Was that a positive or negative learning experience?
2. How have you influenced your children about trusting? If you could do it again and knowing what you now know, would you have parented them differently regarding trust?
3. There's an old equation that you are urged to consider journaling or conversing: "Trust equals faith." Your thoughts?

Hope is an embrace of the unknown.

—*Rebecca Solnit*

CHAPTER THIRTY-ONE

On Taking Risks

How do you handle this matter of risk? Do you carefully weigh all the consequences before you make a choice? Or, do you rush in where angels fear to tread and make those hard decisions despite the results? Or, are you like the fellow who, when asked, "Do you have a hard time making decisions?" said, "Well, yes and no." Most of us fall somewhere in between.

How are you taking those risks in life? Use your imagination for just a moment. If you were stranded in the desert and came across the following letter, which, according to legend, was found in a small baking powder can wired to the handle of an old pump along a long and seldom-used trail in the Amargosa Desert in Nevada. According to this legend, the letter in this can was the only opportunity to get water from this pump.

Though we do not know the source of this note, it had been put there by a man who knew how to survive in the desert. He knew that you not only had to know some of the dangers of the desert but also needed to be ready to help others. And so he was doing just that. He put that note in that can on how to operate that old pump, and the message read as follows:

> This pump is all right as of June, 1932. I put a new sucker washer into it, which ought to last five years. But the washer dries out, and the pump has to be primed. Under the white rock, I buried a bottle of water out of the sun, cork-end up. There's enough water to prime the pump,

but not if you drink some first. Pour about 1/3 and let it soak to wet the leather. Then pour the rest medium fast and pump as hard and fast as possible. You'll get water. The well has never run dry. Have faith. And when you get enough water, fill the bottle, and put it back as you found it for the next feller. Signed, Desert Pete. PS. Don't go drinking up the water first. Prime the pump with it, and you will get all the water you can hold.[24]

"Have faith," Desert Pete says. "Trust that there is some water down there that you can't see. Have faith."

If you were in the desert, what would you have done? Would you have taken that water that you could see? It wasn't enough, but it was a little. Drink it, but it would give no hope to those who came after you. Or, would you have risked wasting that water to prime that pump for unseen water that would be enough for you and all those who came after you? How are you when it comes to the matter of risk?

That letter by Desert Pete is a parable of our lives, leading to the text that Paul wrote to the Philippians. But he also is writing to us: "Keep on working with fear and trembling to complete your salvation, because God is always at work in you."

There are four simple things. First, we need to know that if trying to be secure and safe is our primary goal in life, then being born is a fundamental mistake. God has placed us in a world where we keep stumbling across these baking powder cans called risks—choices that we must make and have to decide. You can't live in this world without taking risks and making difficult choices.

Another thing that must go in our creed and our decision-making is that all these risks and all these choices have consequences. Some are hard, some simple, sometimes profound, and many have lasting implications. Like Jesus, there are unavoidable "Jerusalems" between where we are and where we want to be. But those "Jerusalems" must be confronted, as did Jesus. And most of us would be more ready to act if we had more guarantees of the consequences. But, like Jesus, we don't have those guarantees, and sometimes the results can be the cross.

The third thing: because of those two things, many of us decide to save ourselves by taking as few risks as possible. But we need to know that this security is the worst risk.

When a good cause comes along, and the person must stand up, the person who plays for safety and little consequence will say, "Be careful what you say. Don't say anything that will make waves." But we're in deep trouble when we become more concerned about our necks than our souls.

A relationship is broken, and both wonder who will take the risk. Someone has to. There is a distance between them now. Who caused the break? Was it him? Was it her? Now, they act politely to each other. But neither one takes any risk. They touch but without too much contact. They speak to each other, but they don't share. They talk about everything except what they feel. They smile at one another but never laugh. Why won't they break down and open up? Is it because they do not want to be vulnerable to each other's response? to the other person's possible rejection? To the honesty? To the hurt?

Fourth and last, the good news for some of us struggling with risk and potential failure is that we don't always have to be successful, but we are called to be faithful. You can write this down as the summary of all this teachable moment has tried to suggest: "It is better to fail in a cause that will ultimately triumph than to triumph in any cause that will ultimately fail."[25]

Suggested scripture reading for this lesson: Philippians 3:1–10

Questions for Journaling and Conversation

1. Can you recall risking, and it turned out to be worthwhile?
2. Can you recall risking, and it turned out to be a disaster?
3. Imagine yourself on a trapeze swing with no net below you. The objective is to transfer from the swing you are on to the swing of the "catcher." As this is transpiring, what feelings can you imagine having?

4. You swing into the hands of your "catcher," also swinging on a trapeze swing. He is waiting to catch you, but you must let go and unthinkingly turn to be caught. It is critical that your two swings be in harmony. Would you unthinkingly let go of the security of your swing and then turn, believing that the one to catch you will be there?

CHAPTER THIRTY-TWO:
Visions For A Peaceful Heart

Dr. George Ingalls wrote an article published in the *Annals of Internal Medicine* titled "Sudden and Rapid Death from Psychological Stress." The article reports the results of a study of persons who died after receiving some distressing news. His article reaffirms what the New Testament says: our minds, given to us by God, are miraculous and have a great deal of power over the behavior of our bodies.

> Panic has been described as the ultimate enemy of the human spirit. Whether or not panic is the first thing that can happen to us, it's certainly a close second. Panic can play havoc with our heads, causing us to cringe when we need courage—causing us to throw in the towel at the very time we need to hang in there, forcing us to make a lot of foolish, self-defeating mistakes at the same time. Panic can cause us to give up, run, and retreat when we need to standfast.[26]

Is panic contagious? Is it a viral illness that we catch from one another? Several years ago, I attended a high school football game in Monterey Park, a suburb of Los Angeles. Four spectators, during a game, reported that they were nauseous and vomiting and felt faint. A quick conclusion was made that there was food poisoning from the orange drink at the snack bar because of some copper wiring. Because the loudspeakers weren't working, they instructed the cheerleaders to go before the bleachers and tell the crowd not to drink the orange drink because food poisoning was suspected.

Nearly two hundred people reported being nauseous within a few minutes and began to vomit and faint. Ambulances and private cars were rushing people to the hospital emergency rooms. But it was all a false alarm. While the doctors all found them suffering from symptoms of food poisoning, when they analyzed all the food in that snack bar, they discovered that none of it was contaminated. When the people were told that, their symptoms left them as quickly as they came.

Behavior is indeed contagious. What we put into our minds affects our bodies: garbage in, garbage out. Jesus, in the Gospel Lesson, gives us a vision of who we are. He says, "These things I have spoken to you, and I give you my peace. Not as the world gives. Let not your heart be troubled."

When it comes to our mental and spiritual health, three things come to mind. First, it matters a great deal what we put into our minds. The late Dr. Norman Cousins tells of his experience on a golf course. He noticed an ambulance and paramedics working on a man lying on a stretcher. Because Cousins himself was a survivor of a massive heart attack, he rushed over and noticed that the paramedics were doing what they were trained to do: watching the gauges and gadgets hooked up to the man. But no one was looking at the man.

Cousins looked at the man's face and saw his panic and then saw that the cardiac monitor indicated that his heart rate was so rapid that he was about to go into shock. He went over, put his hand on the man, and said,

"You've got a fine heart."

The man said, "How do you know?"

"I can see on the cardiograph. Furthermore, you're about to be taken to one of the finest hospitals in the nation, and you're going to be just fine."

The man's panic began to subside because something else was going into his mind, and he began to look around and get interested and involved in what was happening.

Dr. Cousins said, "It's a hot day, and you're dehydrated, and that affects the electrical shocks in your heart, and you're going to be all right."[27] He was.

Jesus looked into the people's faces and saw panic, fear, and helplessness. He put his hands on them and said, "Let not your heart be troubled. You're the light of the world! You're the salt of the earth. Claim who you are. Get that in your mind, and then you will know the peace I give."

Second, we have more than one option in a crisis. But we often think our only choice is "Fight, fright, or flight." Francis McNutt, a pioneer in the limitless possibilities of the human spirit, tells a story about his mother and him when he was being willful.

His mother said, "Francis, you have to go stand in that corner."

He did as he was told, but then he said to his mother, "Mother, I refuse to regard this as a corner!"[28]

That's what you and I need to tell ourselves when in a crisis. We have options, and we get to select our emotions and reactions. While we may not change our circumstances, we can choose our attitude toward those circumstances, which will make a difference.

Third, the truth Jesus gives is that we will know his vision for a peaceful heart when we stop thinking that our resources are for our betterment—the "you or me" syndrome. But his vision of peace has the formula of "you and me." I will not have that peace Jesus envisioned unless I share it.

Only when you and I translate our devotions into care and compassion for others do we have a vision of peace that passes all understanding?

Suggested scriptures: Acts 5:1–11; John 14:25–31

Questions for Journaling and Conversation

1. How does the story in the book of Acts apply to this lesson?
2. Have you ever known someone who had lost the will to live?
3. How do we put compassion into practice?

Hope is but the dream of those who wake.

—*Matthew Prior*

CHAPTER THIRTY-THREE

Jealousy

A former client shared this self-realization with me: "There have been four occasions in my life in which I thought I was dying. Once, when I thought I had a terrible illness. The other three times were when I was jealous."

Jealousy can be that deep. It can make you feel as if you want to die. Or it can make you wish that someone else would die. It can go that badly. Indeed, people murder for jealousy. Jealousy constantly produces the passion for a crime we hear so much from police reports.

What does jealousy feel like? That personal hurt pains you when someone you compete with surpasses you or, in someone else's mind, is reaching you. That emotional hurt is jealousy. Just so, that secret elation, gloating, and almost rejoicing that we feel when someone we've competed with stumbles, makes a mistake, drops the baton, falls, or suffers some misfortune ... that's also jealousy. Who was it that said, "Why is it easier to sympathize with your friends in their sorrow than it is to exalt with them in their joy?"

Jealousy. It casts a long shadow. And it's painful because it usually operates with those we're familiar with. A physician is generally not jealous of a pharmacist but of another physician. A teacher with another teacher. It's usually found among our colleagues, friends, and families. And it is the one emotion from which we get no pleasure. The only thing we get from jealousy is torment.

Is there any hope we can hold on to? Can jealousy be redeemed and transformed? Is there any way that jealousy can become what Paul said he had: "divine jealousy"? Can it listen to, talk to, or learn from it?

First, try not to feel so guilty about jealousy, be ashamed, or try to hide it. I don't know anyone who has ever cured, redeemed or transformed their jealousy by denying or repressing it. Listen to it. Talk to it. That's the only way you'll ever tame it.

Second, if we listen to our jealousy, we can discover what's underneath it. In some ways, jealousy is the feeling; it's the cover-up for things underneath. Other fears, for example, that jealousy may be hiding, perhaps even the oldest fear of all: the fear of being abandoned, the fear of being forsaken, the fear of losing control of the other person. Look *under* your jealousy.

In the Hebrew Testament, the first commandment is "Thou shalt have no other gods before me." But we often forget the rest of the commandment: "For I am a jealous God." As the Bible unfolds, the jealousy of God is that we will lose our relationship with God by putting other gods before Yahweh. The damage will be more to ourselves, not to God. "I am a jealous God because of what idolatry will do to you."

God regards us as sacred, and that's what makes jealousy holy. If we could see the person where jealousy exists and view them as holy, religious, or a child of God, our jealousy would also become sacred and holy. It may mean you must go to that person, not with accusation but with communication. You may risk destroying the relationship, but then again, you may deepen it.

This story is from the ages:

> A young couple went to a restaurant with their five-year-old son. The waitress took the order for the adults, then turned to the little boy and said, "Now, son, what will you have?"
>
> Not being used to being treated like that, he said, "I'll have a hot dog!"

Immediately, his mother approached him and said, "No, he won't. He will have meat and potatoes and mixed vegetables."

But this was not the kind of waitress who could be intimidated by any mortal, let alone a parent. She continued her conversation with the boy and said, "And, son, what will you have on that hot dog?"

"Mustard!" he cried out, "and lots of it!"

And then she said, "Coming up!" and walked away.

The little boy turned to his parents and said, "Gee, she thinks I'm real!"

That's what God thinks about us. God is in love with us but is in trouble with us because God thinks we're honest. God's jealousy is holy because God regards us as sacred. That's the only thing that redeems us. And our jealousy can become holy if we regard that other person as real or sacred. And then it becomes another story.

Questions for Journaling and Conversation

1. What color is jealousy? How does that color describe jealousy for you?
2. Take a few moments and journal who you were jealous of and why.
3. Does it make sense to challenge ourselves to see that person as holy or sacred because then the jealousy becomes sacred or holy? This is versus "demonizing" the person we are so jealous of.
4. Does jealousy have any redeeming purpose?

Hope is the only thing stronger than fear.

—Robert Ludlum

CHAPTER THIRTY-FOUR:
Expectations

W e begin a review on this subject with two parables: Jesus told and God told. First, the one God told. It's called the Parable of the Crab.

Crabs are fascinating creatures. To be secure, they create a shell around them, which is their security. But God has so made them as God has made us that the crab continues to grow, but the shell doesn't. And if the crab doesn't destroy the body, get out of it, and make a new one, the crab will die. The crab must destroy the old shell and wait until a new one is created. And it is at this time that the crab is most vulnerable. This may be why some crabs create new shells so strong that when it comes time to shed and break this shell, they can't, and, eventually, it destroys them.

Now, let's introduce Jesus's experience with a crab. A lawyer disguised as a crab.

"Teacher," the lawyer said, "what must I do to inherit eternal life?" He said to him, "What is written in the law? What do you read there?" He answered, "You shall love the Lord your God with all your heart and soul and with all your strength and mind, and your neighbor as yourself.

Jesus knew the lawyer knew the answer. It's almost a rhetorical question posed by both men. But then the lawyer goes deeper and asks a question that has haunted the laws of civility for centuries: "But, Rabbi, just who is my neighbor?" Behind this spoken question was an unspoken question. The real question.

Jesus knew this, so Jesus used the art of story to drive home His point. And He tells the lawyer about that road that led from Jerusalem to Jericho and all that happened there. We have all heard this story many times, but a good story bears repeating.

> "A man was going down from Jerusalem to Jericho and fell into the hands of robbers, who stripped him, beat him, and went away, leaving him half dead. Now by chance a priest was going down that road; and when he saw him, he passed by on the other side. So likewise a Levite, when he came to the place and saw him, passed him by on the other side.
>
> "But a Samaritan while traveling came near him; and when he saw him, he was moved with pity. He went to him and bandaged his wounds, having poured oil and wine on them. Then he put him on his own animal, brought him to an inn, and took care of him.
>
> "The next day he took out two denarii, gave them to the innkeeper, and said, 'Take care of him, and when I come back, I will repay you whatever more you spend.' Which of these three do you think, was a neighbor to the man who fell into the hands of the robbers?" The lawyer said, "The one who showed him mercy." Jesus said to him, "Go and do likewise." (Luke 10:25–37)

Earlier in the book, I shared the story of a client who once was a decathlete. He could do it all. But, one day, while on his roof cleaning the troughs for a storm, he fell off that roof and was suddenly a quadriplegic. I asked him how he learned to cope with such a dramatic change in his life. He said, "The first thing I had to do was adjust. The second thing I had to do was adjust. And the third thing I had to do was adjust."

Can you identify with that? How many adjustments can you make before you crumble? How many changes can a person handle in a lifetime? How many changes can a person endure in one year? Living can be hazardous to our health.

We don't have to live long to know that the walking wounded and the human wreckage is all around us—people who have yet to acquire the skill of adjusting, adjusting, adjusting. Crabs that build bigger and more formidable shells around themselves threaten their welfare instead of protecting them. That's the first teachable moment.

The second teachable moment from these two parables is that if we're going to bend and not break, we need to learn how to sacrifice our expectations of ourselves and other people. When the lawyer asked Jesus, "What is expected of me?" Jesus knew he wasn't asking, "How can I be more compassionate?" but "How can I stay in more control?"; not "How can I go through life being of more service?" but "How can I go through life being more secure?" "Tell me, who is my neighbor? What is expected of me?"

Three people come along—all with expectations of getting to Jericho safely. But only one of the three sacrifices his expectations. Only one is willing to lay down his original intentions for what he planned to do and be open to the actual situation before him.

How do we translate this into our lives? One of the most common complaints among families and friends is that you're too busy to listen. We become so locked in on what we're going to do that we refuse to sacrifice our expectations to see what is happening to those around us. We will abandon sacrificing for others so that we can stay in control.

But to bend without breaking, as individuals and as a church, we must commit to sacrificing our expectations and get past the illusion of building a security system that will be impenetrable.

One last teachable moment: it has to do with the low expectations that we have of ourselves, the low opinions we have of ourselves. As a therapist, this is a significant component of our well-being.

I am a fan of writer Dr. A. J. Cronin. Before he was a writer, he was a medical doctor. He attended medical school in London and was assigned to assist a very skilled and well-known surgeon. But this surgeon was impatient with anyone less than perfect and constantly derided Cronin's performance. "You'll never make it as a surgeon." And this just added to Cronin's already low opinion of himself.

Upon getting his medical degree, he was assigned to be the only physician in a small village in the highlands of Scotland. He was their doctor, except when it came to surgery. He did not have the confidence to be their surgical doctor.

One time, around the Christmas season, a terrible snowstorm shut the village off from the rest of the world. The local minister's son was chopping down a tree, which fell across the boy's back and crushed him. When Cronin examined him, he determined that he had several crushed vertebrae, which caused the boy to be paralyzed. He would need emergency surgery, but there was no way to get the boy to a surgeon because of the storm, and all Cronin thought about was that surgeon sneering and saying, "You'll never make it as a surgeon."

Cronin said to the boy's family, "There's nothing that can be done." But the father of the boy and minister to Cronin said most humbly, "Yes, there is, and you can do it. And God expects you to do it, and God will be with you."

Cronin, in his autobiography, described what happened next. "My hand grew steady, and I felt power flow into me. I made the incision and worked only by a sense of touch on the crushed vertebrae. At the end of the hour, I saw the boy's legs slowly move.

Tears of joy and relief fill my eyes. I walked into the next room and told the family, 'He'll live. He'll walk again.'"[29]

We need to move out from our shells of security that keep us from bending to what is before us. We must sacrifice our low opinions and expectations of ourselves to move into a trust that we might be open and notice the meaning of the moment.

If you hear yourself, say, "I don't have the skills to get involved in that problem (and you can name the problem), and there's nothing I can do," instead, listen to your heart and soul: "Yes, there is, and you can do it. God expects you to do it and will be with you!"

Suggested scripture: Luke 10:25–37

Questions for Journaling and Conversation

1. Do you have any comments on this lesson?
2. How does the Parable of the Crab speak to you?
3. How does the Parable of the Good Samaritan apply to us personally and corporately?
4. Where do you get your validation?

CHAPTER THIRTY-FIVE:

You Don't Have To Know Who You Are

This story is easy to love because all of us experience the feeling of loss. How do you define "lostness"? Does it include events you read in today's paper? Does it cover the pain of the world? Is your definition large enough and broad enough so that all of us can park our tragedies inside of it?

Lostness. It often comes in the form of fear, anxiety, or worry.

It is often filled with disappointment and uncertainty. Loss reminds us of how little control we have, and that can overwhelm us.

How do sheep get lost? They nibble themselves away from the herd. A little clump of grass here and a little there, and they fail to look up at the shepherd, and before long, when they do look up, the shepherd is nowhere in sight. That's why the Bible says, "All we like sheep have gone astray."

That's how relationships are lost. That's how friendships are lost. That's how marriages are lost. We nibble them away. The sarcastic smile, a flippant remark, a brisk denial, a bitter sigh—so small, hardly worth noting, forgetting, or forgiving. And one day, we look up, and the relationship is lost.

What would he do if a man had a hundred sheep and lost one? We love that story because we experience this same sense of "lostness" in many ways.

This story also reminds us that we can't be our own shepherd. We can't be, therefore, our own savior. We spend so much time trying to understand who we are. We are indeed a complexity of selves. We have a generous self and a selfish self. There's our jealous self, our gracious self, our pious self, and our passionate self.

The Psalmist asks in Psalm 8 the same question and speaks to the one at the heart of it all: "What is man that thou art mindful of him?" And what insight did he come up with? "You have made us a little lower than the angels and just a little above the animals." And where did he gain this insight? From *The Book of Genesis*. Here, we learn how it all started, and no one has yet to improve it.

One day, God reached down and took a little clod of dirt, formed it and shaped it, then bent down and gave it mouth-to-mouth resuscitation (the Bible is more poetic). And God blew spirit into it, and it became a living soul.

That's who we are. We're part heaven and part earth. We're part angel and part animal. It's all running through our veins…jealousy, love, caring, and selfishness. It's all there. Part angel, part animal. Part earth, part heaven. So, who are we? We may never fully answer that question.

The good news is that while we may never fully find ourselves, we must be located. The Christian faith is the only faith that says we have a God who seeks us.

Jesus said in his story, "What man of you, if you had a hundred sheep, and one of them was lost, will not go after it?" Not a man there would. We play the percentages. Lose one out of a hundred? That's good business sense. But Jesus is saying that God doesn't play the percentages. Even one, God will use all of eternity to see and find that one lost sheep. We may not know who we are, but we can know *whose* we are.

A summary of Jesus's story: Jacques Cousteau says that when a baby porpoise Is born, not just the mother but also other porpoises will swim underneath the newborn and slowly lift it above the water so it can breathe again.[30]

God doesn't ask much more of us than of the porpoise. There will be people around us who may think they are going down for the last time. To be a disciple of Jesus is to be willing to be God's everlasting arms to those who need a lifting up for a little while so they can breathe. Perhaps someone will do it for you. God asks from us nothing more but doesn't ask anything less.

Suggested scripture: Luke 15:1–7

Questions for Journaling and Conversation

1. What additional characteristics come to mind when it comes to defining ourselves?
2. Willie Lohman defended his behavior by declaring, "I have a right to find out who I am!" Did he?
3. Take a few moments and, with pen and paper, write the phrase ten times: "I am …" and then complete each phrase.

CHAPTER THIRTY-SIX

Hope Restored

A Concluding Teachable Moment

Hope can hinge upon the most unlikely of carriers. Watching how hope can restore a person's passion for living to the fullest, even though they have only a few months to live, is an exceptional kind of hope.

The beginning of this next story takes place in a children's cancer ward. One particular room is occupied by Paul, a sixteen-year-old boy diagnosed with cancer who had just undergone surgery to amputate his left leg.

Amputating the leg of a sixteen-year-old is to expect serious consequences. Paul was a popular student, basketball player, honor roll, handsome, and outgoing. He was a gifted young man with a bright future until his diagnosis.

He came out of the surgery and went into a deep depression. No one could get him to talk about the surgery or anything else.

He was almost catatonic. He shut himself off from the rest of the world. Even his mother couldn't reach him or his doctor. He just stared at the ceiling and blocked out everything around him. That is when he became my next patient.

I sat down beside his bed and introduced myself. "Paul, my name is Dr. Bill Stephenson, and I'm a counselor. I work only with kids like you who are facing a life-threatening illness. I can help you through this, but only if you want to. At least think about it, and I'll check in on you later. OK?"

Paul just looked up at the ceiling with no emotion shown. I got up and met his mom standing in the hallway.

"Dr. Stephenson, I am at my wit's end. He won't even speak to me and know how hurt I am."

"He's here for a while," I said. "Let's see if we can pull him out of his shell."

Later that day, as was the custom of the ward, all the children in the ward (except infants) were to go to the recreation room to hear stories read and told. I sat on the carpet with several children around me and began telling them a story.

As I began to tell the children a story, I noticed that Paul had been wheeled into the room and was on the margin of my group. But I noticed he was listening intently and watching all the kids reacting to my wild story that spoke of hope and promise. I could tell that Paul listened to every word and watched the children's reactions.

Later that evening, I went into Paul's room. "Paul, you have gone through a tremendous ordeal, and I think you know that there is probably more to come. You will soon be going home, and you're going to have to figure out what you're going to do, and I think you know that you're running out of options."

There was a long period of silence, and then Paul finally spoke.

"This girl had invited me to escort her to the annual spring formal. After my surgery, I received a text saying that she had changed her mind and that I would understand. Yeah, right. I mean, who would want to have a cripple for an escort to a dance!

"Dr. Stephenson, I don't want to go home. My family looks at me, waging a losing battle. My friends treat me as if I have some virus. They fear they might catch it. But today, in the recreation room, I felt safe. I felt as if I belonged here. You know, Bill …"

"Dr. Bill, Paul. Boundaries." He understood.

"Dr. Bill, do you think I could come back and volunteer? I love reading and telling stories. I know I could do what I saw you doing today. Do you think?"

"You would need some training, but Paul, I think you would be a terrific volunteer. Let me make it happen."

"Fantastic! Now I have a reason to get up in the morning! When can I start?"

"Tomorrow. Why don't you think about a story you could tell, and I'll yield the floor to you? If it works, you can come back anytime when you go home. But, Paul, would you be willing to work with me to smooth things out at home? Consider bringing a few of your friends together for a serious conversation."

"Sure. And thanks, Dr. Bill."

"What for, Paul?"

"For giving me back my hope."

Paul would return and become the best reader and storyteller ever. He was like a Pied Piper to the children. And he came back every single day! Even when he was sick, he could be seen wheeling his chair onto the ward. And the moment he came on the ward, the children would immediately wend their way to the recreation room, anticipating Paul's hour of story. They would put his chair in the middle of the circle and then give him books to read, but Paul would often have a story to tell, usually one that he had written himself, about a boy with one leg. The kids idolized him.

Every day! Four months passed when Paul came onto the ward for the last time. Not in a wheelchair but in an ER mobile bed. He was so sick, in pain, and weak—no more storytelling in the recreation room. But that didn't deter the kids. They would sneak into his room and put books on his bed. "Paul, would you read us this story?" "Paul, this is a short book. Could you read it to us?"

And, somehow, Paul would find the strength to read to these children as they sat around his bed. And, each day, we would see the children circling his bed. And when he could no longer read to them, they kept sneaking into his room, circling his bed, and reading stories to each other—I want to think to Paul as well.

One night, a divine hope descended upon him, and he was gone. Paul thought his life was ending when they amputated his leg. In a sense, it did come to an end, but he found a new life, a new beginning, and he came to live it passionately to the very end. Paul had a defining hope.

May the testimonies shared in this book inspire and encourage you to restore your hope—for yourself and those you care about and care about you.

Questions for Journaling and Conversation

1. Can you think of a different definition when "hope equals cure" no longer works?
2. Have you ever had a time when you felt you had lost hope? If so, write this out and be prepared to share it.
3. Have you ever assisted someone in restoring their hope?

Hope is like a star:

Not to be seen in the sunshine of prosperity

And only to be discovered in the night of adversity.

—Charles Spurgeon

AFTERWORD:
What I Have Learned From My Teachable Moments

1.   When you're in love, it shows.

2.   When someone says to me, "You've made my day!" it makes my day.

3.   Being kind is more important than being right.

4.   Never say no to a gift from a child.

5.   Everyone needs a friend to act goofy with.

6.   Sometimes, the most we can do is to be there to hold a hand and listen.

7.   Ignoring the facts does not change them.

8.   Getting even with someone is letting the person continue to hurt me.

9.   Love, not time, heals all wounds.

10. No one is perfect until you fall in love with them.

11. Life is tough, but I am tougher.

12. When I harbor bitterness and resentment, inner peace will dock elsewhere.

13. Happiness is not at the top. It's in the climb.

14. The less time I have to work with, the more things I get done.

15. I cannot change the past, but I can change the meaning the past has for me.

ACKNOWLEDGMENTS

The material in this book was three years in the making. But it would need a "testing ground" to see if the material was relevant to the topic I was writing about. A group of men and women I had come to love and trust, agreed to use the material as a launching pad for discussion and self-examination. And it was a success.

I want to acknowledge how valuable they were in keeping me focused on bringing material that enabled them to reach for and attain a higher level of understanding of themselves and God's involvement in their lives.

I also want to especially acknowledge my wife, Carol. I would spend long hours each week developing the material for the book but also developing it in such a way as others could use it in a group format. She was the first one to read and critique the material that would be implemented in the group and eventually become known as *Teachable Moments*.

I would like to thank Writers' Branding for their significant contribution to the quality and production of this book.

And to the saints whose stories inspired this book. This includes the families, friends and loved ones who enriched and encouraged me to tell and share the courageous and inspirational journey of their loved one's story, and the legacy they were left to carry on to others.

I cannot ethically benefit from the sale of this book. Any profits from the sale of this book will go to support children and youth who find themselves in desperate situations.

—Bill Stephenson

BIBLIOGRAPHY

1. What Does God Know, You Tube, May 25, 2023.

2. Twentieth Century Studios, December 15, 2020, Bob Clark, Dir.

3. "Ivan Goodman," San Francisco Chronicle, July 1, 1943.

4. This person wished to remain anonymous.

5. Guest of the Revolution, by Kathryn Koob, T. Nelson Publisher, 1982, pp. 132-133.

6. "Kohlberg's Stages of Moral Development", Frameworks and Theories, August 17, 2020.

7. Adventures of Huckleberry Finn, by Mark Twain, Published in America, 1885, Chapter 11.

8. Motivation and Personality, by A.H. Maslow, Harper Row, New York, 1954.

9. Psychology of Habit, by William James, 1887.

10. The Lessons of John Wesley, by John Elford, ed. London Epworth Publishing, 1931, chap. 13.

11. Care Enough to Confront by David Augsburger, Revell Publishing, 1973.

12. "Speech in Defense of His Doctrines of the Diet of Worms," by Martin Luther, Apr.18, 1521.

13. The Concept of Anxiety, 1844, by Soren Kierkegaard, English Trans., 1944, by Walter Laurie, p 26.

14. Death of the Creative Life, by L.H. Goodman, Springer Publications, 2nd edition, 1981, p. 77.

15. The Book of Joy, by the Dalai Lama, Desmond Tutu, and Douglas Abrams. Random House, 2016, p.466.

16. Necessary Losses, by Judith Viorst. Simon & Schuster, 2002, p. 197.

17. Power! How to Get it, How to Use It, by Michael Korda, Grand Central Pub., January 1991, p. 233.

18. Learning to Fly, by Sam Keen. Harmony Publishing, May 11, 1999, p. 256.

19. "A Drunken Fatality and Forgiveness," by the Associated Press. Published In the New York Times, April 22, 1985, section B, p. 13.

20. "Freddie Steinmark: Make a Wish For Him," Los Angeles Times, June 8, 1996, Sports section, p. 7.

21. "Bruce Gardner Commits Suicide," Los Angeles Times, June 8, 1996, Sports Section, p. 7.

22. Private Battle, by Cornelius and Kathryn Ryan, Simon & Schuster, January 1979.

23. A. Lincoln, by Ronald White, Random House, 2009, pp. 204-205.

24. "Desert Pete," the NBX Press, May 31, 1991. The origin of this piece is not known.

25. "Inaugural Speech," by Woodrow Wilson, Jan. 1916.

26. "Death From Psychological Stress," by George Ingalls, MD, Oct. 2004.

27. The Healing Heart: Antidotes to Panic and Helplessness, Avon Books, 1984, p. 221.

28. Healing, by Francis McNutt, Ave Maria Press, Jan. 1, 1999, pp. 129-130.

29. The Man Who Created Dr. Finley, by Allen Davis. Anna Books Publishing, May 15, 2011, pp. 228-229.

30. Whales, by Jacque-Yves Cousteau, New York, Abrams Publishing, 1988.

www.ingramcontent.com/pod-product-compliance
Lightning Source LLC
Chambersburg PA
CBHW051520120626
46551CB00012B/1010